In Search  of You

Letters to a daughter

Patsy Freeman

Matador
9 Priory Business Park,
Wistow Road, Kibworth Beauchamp,
Leicestershire. LE8 0RX
Tel: 0116 279 2299
Email: books@troubador.co.uk
Web: www.troubador.co.uk/matador
Twitter: @matadorbooks

ISBN 978 1838594 190

British Library Cataloguing in Publication Data.
A catalogue record for this book is available from the British Library.

Printed and bound by CPI Group (UK) Ltd, Croydon, CR0 4YY
Typeset in 11.5pt Adobe Garamound by Troubador Publishing Ltd, Leicester, UK

Matador is an imprint of Troubador Publishing Ltd

For those treading the courageous path through grief, I honour and salute you. Let us reach out to one another and stand together, for together we are stronger.

Contents

Part One

Before

Dearest Jasmine,

Muppet hears your car before I do and he begins barking in the hallway. It's what he always does, though from the moment you step through the door it is clear something is wrong. Usually, you drop to your knees to wrestle with Muppet, fondle his ears and stare into his adoring brown eyes. This time, you brush him aside with hardly a word, shake off your jacket and come upstairs. Muppet follows behind at your heels.

I'm still reeling with the news that you have been diagnosed with breast cancer, so goodness knows how you are feeling. It's ten days since your hospital appointment and I've been longing for you to come round. Well, actually I've been feeling nervous as I'm not sure how you will be. I make tea for us and we sit on the sofa. Muppet jumps up between us, but you barely stroke him. The tea is too hot so you rest it on the table. I notice you've bitten your nails, but only on your right hand. I do that sometimes. I'm not expecting you to be this composed. Your eyes have a faraway look which tells me you are in shock, and you are edgy and a bit guarded. You go over to the window, brush your hair back from your face and although it's not cold, you wrap your cardigan around you. This is too much, way too much after everything else you've been through. I want to weep, but I don't. I won't ask too many questions.

Love,

Mum

Jasmine,

Another night of not sleeping. How on earth are we going to manage this?

You didn't tell me when you found the lump in your breast, but you contacted your sister, Emma. And of course you know Emma will tell me. It's been like this for years. Either you tell Emma something or you tell me, but you never tell both of us. The dynamics between the three of us are clumsy. Sometimes I do or say something that annoys or upsets you; however, I never find out what it is because you don't tell me. I'm not even sure you know. At other times, there are misunderstandings between you and Emma. What I find interesting is that you never fall out with both of us. In other words, when Emma is out of favour, I am in favour. And vice versa. Don't you think that a little strange? Your father doesn't enter into the equation. I think you and he had a big argument. I'm not sure. Anyway, you see very little of each other.

At times, I try to broach the subject of the strange dynamics going on between the three of us, but the topic is never fully aired, because you usually get annoyed or else you leave. Your father reckons you are plain awkward. Emma says I should be firmer with you. I guess I just want peace between us without worrying about what I am going to say to you.

Emma went with you for your first appointment at the

hospital. It's a way for her to travel. She is very kind and capable and I know she will find a way to quietly take charge of this delicate situation. She will accompany you to your hospital appointments. So often the eldest child is brought up to be the responsible one. It was the same for me growing up with two younger brothers.

As children you and Emma loved acting and role-playing. Emma takes charge and her favourite role is playing the part of the headmistress, which means you are her pupil. Sometimes there is a riot when you insist on having a turn at being the head!

So Emma going with you to the hospital is a relief, though I must admit part of me feels a little left out. Anyway, this is not straightforward, that much I'm sure of. Nothing is normal anymore. You look well, but you are anything but. You have cancer, for goodness sake, and the tumour is too big for surgery. You are now a patient, with a hospital number and a brown folder that will no doubt get thicker over the months. I can't believe this. How are we going to deal with this, Jasmine?

It is a relief when you tell me the treatment you have decided upon.

'Mum, I've decided not to have chemotherapy. I don't think my body is strong enough to cope with it. I've been to see my GP and he will start me on mistletoe injections. Apparently, mistletoe has good results with cancer. I'll also have a course of acupuncture to calm my body down, and we can look up some supplements to boost my immune system.' I nod. You have my full support.

The consultant not surprisingly wants you to have chemotherapy and he also tells you that you might die without it. How does that make you feel? Without hesitating, you ask him not to talk about dying again.

How dare the lump land in your beautiful body.

Love,

Mum

Darling,

You had your first injection of mistletoe yesterday. Your arm swells and is quite painful afterwards. Mistletoe is very much in line with the remedies used by the indigenous to treat cancer. When I was in Ecuador in 2004, I was fortunate indeed to meet the chief of an indigenous tribe. For me, it was a dream come true, as for many years I have held the indigenous in high regard. Meeting Chief Antul was not quite by chance though, because the manager of the hostel where I was staying happens to be a friend of his. And Antul just happens to be in town when the manager phones him to say that someone would love to meet him.

The young chief is in his late thirties and is wearing blue jeans and a black t-shirt. His long, dark hair is tied back in a braid. He is drop-dead gorgeous, Jasmine! The manager brings him over and introduces us. One of Antul's first questions is to ask me why I am interested in his people. How do I tell him in Spanish that the way the indigenous see the world makes complete sense to me – that we are all connected energetically and that all living things are sacred, including the rocks, plants, animals and trees? My Spanish stumbles yet we end up talking for two hours. I am lost for words when Antul invites me to spend two weeks with his people in the jungle. I was not expecting any of this. He tells me conditions will be basic as there is no electricity and all washing takes place in the river. I carry on nodding, still unable to believe what is taking place. Finally, we negotiate a price and say goodnight.

Jasmine, I hardly sleep a wink that night in case I am making a big mistake and might never return to England. I email you and Emma, giving you no cause for concern, with the name of the hostel where I hope to be returning.

True to his word, Antul is there first thing in the morning. He takes my rucksack and slings it over his shoulder, informing me we will be travelling most of the day. We catch two different buses, both heading east towards the Amazon Jungle. The Amazon River is majestic! I stand watching it glinting and snaking into the distance. Four of us, along with a goat, get on board a small flatboat cranked by chains to cross us over to the other side. A bus is waiting to pick us up, and after that there is just a local taxi ride. The whole thing has been seamless. We reach a gateway to the jungle. 'It will be two more hours,' Antul informs me. We are getting to know each other and I'm looking forward to meeting his wife Elsa, and their three children.

Our trek through the jungle was extraordinary, alive with colour, sounds, huge trees and birdsong; yet the biggest noise of all, he tells me, comes from a spider on the ground.

I'm relieved and tired when we arrive, and pleased that no one makes a fuss of me. I liked Elsa from the moment we met. She and Antul were the only ones who speak Spanish. The others talk in their own dialect. Elsa showed me to my round wooden hut with about twelve wooden beds in it. I chose the bed nearest the window. Six families occupied the other four huts, so I felt somewhat embarrassed to have one all to myself.

Jasmine, I remember telling you about their welcome ceremony. The men, women and children were all dressed in ceremonial red, and their cheeks were painted with two red stripes made from berry juice. One of the women offered to paint my cheeks too. They all began dancing and singing and one of the men invited me to join in. Then I was served a meal of wild turkey and green leaves that resembled spinach. It tasted wonderful. Antul explained that the soul of the turkey was blessed and the animal thanked for giving its life. It was the first time I'd eaten meat in years and it tasted delicious!

During the course of the two weeks, I get a real feel for the way the women take care of the women and the men look after the men. Naturally, I spend most of the time with the women. The fishing trip without a rod or a line was truly memorable. It was a two-hour walk to the river, and on the way they stopped and sang over recently planted trees and sweet potato crops to encourage their growth. When we reached the river, the women began cutting down some bulbous roots with machete knives. They then bashed the ends against the rocks with a large flat stone, whilst another woman held out a wooden bowl to catch the dripping white fluid. She then carefully poured the juice into the river to temporarily mesmerise the fish. There was a lovely rhythm in the way they went about this. My attempts at catching a fish with my hands were in vain, which seemed to amuse them very much!

Jasmine, I remember the day I spent with Elsa looking at plants growing in the jungle. It has me thinking about your mistletoe treatment. She introduced me to a whole range of plants that are remedies for different ailments. There is a bush with small red berries that provides the women with contraception. Elsa pointed out a plant for diarrhoea and sickness, and another to calm the nerves. Now here's a thing:

the remedy for cancer is a juice extracted from the bark of a tree known as "dragon's blood". You take five drops daily, and it is so powerful that when it is used on a wound, the wound heals within two days. So you may imagine what I'm going to suggest now, Jasmine.

'Would you like to visit these people? We could go together. I know it's a long way to travel, but what do you think? Perhaps we might go sooner rather than later.'

You reflect a little and then shake your head. Ah, I see how tired you are. Your guard is coming down. You poor darling. You tell me the combination of mistletoe, acupuncture and supplements are enough for now, and a friend has recommended someone we can go to for healing. It's a bit of a distance away but frankly, you do anything if it will help.

I hope you are managing to get some sleep.

Love,

Mum

Sweetheart,

How are you in yourself? You don't share very much. I'm grateful for Muppet's company, though I feel very alone. How are we going to manage this?

Emma lives two and a half hours away and she is busy with work and of course looking after Josh, who is fourteen years old, and Penny, who is ten. Emma will be able to take you to the hospital for your appointments. You never talk about your father and I don't know if you've even told him about the cancer, though I'm sure Emma has. You are not in touch with him so this is all up to me. It's always been like that, right from when we were first married.

We were very young. I was only twenty and Alan twenty-three. I suppose I just followed the old paradigms that I saw playing out with my parents, and Alan did the same with his. We were in that sense a perfect match. It meant that I took care of you and Emma and the home, while Alan's priority was his work. Unlike Alan's mother, however, who did not have a job, I did. I explained to Alan over and over that I couldn't manage to do everything myself. I asked him for more help. He didn't appear to hear me. But then I managed to cope, so he didn't need to hear me.

These old ways are changing. The family living next door to me have two little girls. The parents seem to share most things. That must be so nice. Emma and Charlie also do things differently and I am pleased to see how well they communicate with each other.

How long is it since they met? It must be nigh on twenty years. Do you remember on Boxing Day tucking yourself behind the curtain at the front window to get a view of Charlie as he approached the house? Just two days earlier, on Christmas Eve, Emma wanted to go out, so she and a friend went to the one and only nightclub in town. Emma danced with any number of people. The next day someone called Charlie phones; however, Emma can't remember anything about him! I imagine a few glasses of wine were consumed that night. Emma asks you to position yourself at the window so you can tell her what Charlie looks like.

'It's okay, Emma. Open the door. He's gorgeous!' So Charlie was let into the house. Those were such carefree days. We didn't know how lucky we were. You never do. It's not like that now. The rug has been well and truly pulled out from under us. I would much rather it was me going through this than you, and I don't like the fact that you live on your own. Oh dear, I'm all over the place. I forgot to ask when you will be going for another appointment at the hospital. Emma will tell me.

What happens now? Does life just carry on while we wait to see how you get on? I expect you are in bed now.

Love,

Mum

Jasmine,

I'm not sleeping very well. You probably aren't either. You are usually grumpy when I phone, and when you don't answer, I leave a message. I don't want to crowd you. I've found some good films on DVD which I think you'll enjoy. I'll bring them over, but I have difficulty hearing on your laptop as the sound is so poor. Tomorrow, you're coming over for supper so perhaps we might watch one here. Films are a wonderful tonic amidst everything going on. I'm trying not to fuss too much and I don't know if I have the right balance. I wonder how you are feeling. Up and down I imagine.

I enjoyed going to the healer with you, as it gave us time together. He comes highly recommended so my fingers and toes are crossed. We'll go again. There was a nice clothes shop nearby and you tried on a long, dark blue velvet dress. It looks lovely on you. Your eyes are bright and the shop light shines gold in your hair, the same colour as it was when you were a child. The woman says the dress is more for the summer, but the fact that you consider buying it shows me you are thinking ahead. That's good to see and it reminds me to do the same.

Love,

Mum

Dear Jasmine,

Yesterday's second hospital appointment was very hard. I wasn't there and in some ways I'm glad. It was your thirty-eighth birthday – what a way to spend your birthday. Emma takes the day off work and comes over to fetch you. I'm so glad she is there at your side. You are kept waiting ages and ages for your appointment; three hours, I think Emma said.

The consultant says there is good news. Your tumour is sensitive to hormone treatment, so this will buy you an extra six months of life. What on earth does he mean? And is buying six extra months of life good news? I feel gutted and confused. Is he saying you will die after six months? Are you going to die? I feel stunned. How on earth are you? Emma says you didn't say much. I'm scared. You don't share anything. It's as if there is nothing wrong. I don't want to talk about cancer every time I see you, far from it. It's just that it never gets a mention.

After leaving the hospital, Emma takes you out to an Indian restaurant. She sends across a photo. You are both smiling and raising your beer bottles at the waiter who is taking the picture. You look happy but I don't think you can be. They say the camera doesn't lie. Oh yes, it does. Emma says it was one of the saddest days of her life. Birthdays have always been special in our family, something to celebrate, even when you have breast cancer. I am sad I wasn't there for your birthday, but you, me and

Emma rarely spend time together. I don't understand it. I think I never will.

Sleep evades me. I don't like waking at this hour, as it makes everything seem so much worse. I'm finding this hard.

Thinking of you, sweetheart.

Love,

Mum

Dear Jasmine,

I'm up early, having slept a little better than usual. I shall pop round later this morning. I've made soup and a few other things for you. Thank goodness you only live three miles away – it was so clever of you to find the flat. Imagine how it would be if you were still living in Bournemouth. That was only two years ago. Goodness, look how far you've come in that time. You were doing brilliantly. And now BOOM. Breast cancer. Everything's gone up in smoke.

Two years ago, I drove down to Bournemouth. Your phone call upset me. You want me to go down. You sound dreadful. The nearer I got to you, the worse I felt. Something was definitely up. You took ages answering the door bell, which I've learned is not a good sign. When you finally open the door, your eyes are red and puffy from crying and you have one hand over your stomach, which makes me wonder if you are in pain. You don't want a hug. Instead, you turn and walk slowly up the stairway and I follow you up to your flat.

There is a comfy red armchair in the corner and you sink into it. You no longer hold back the tears. You don't want me to touch you. The room is airless but I don't open a window. Your breathing is too fast and you are getting into a panic. I slow my own breathing down to give you a bit of a rhythm. I've never had a panic attack but I know how scary they are. I talk about nothing very much, wash up some mugs in the sink and put the kettle on. The clatter of crockery is comforting and I find biscuits in a tin. The kettle boils and I bring over two mugs of tea. You shouldn't be on your own in this state.

'What's the matter? What's happened?' And then you begin telling me how buried childhood memories have begun surfacing. You were a child. You think there is a man in the house… he's a friend of ours… and he harms you. The memories come in pieces, a little jumbled up. Talking about this causes you to shrink back. You look dreadful. Your hair is a little greasy and your nails are bitten down the sides. We finish our tea and I suggest a walk down to the sea. It's not far. We gather up our coats. It's good to be outside. I feel cold, but not because of the weather. Standing side by side, we watch a glorious streak of orange turning darker in the sky and then a few stars appear.

When did your concerns about your childhood start? Ah yes, it was soon after you left college, so you would have been twenty-two. That was the first time you asked me whether something awful happened to you as a child. I was surprised by your question and couldn't think of anything. There was the time you were bullied in the school playground, but I don't think it was traumatic and you went back to school the next day.

'No, it wasn't that.' You shook your head and the little creases deepened between your brows.

The subject was dropped until a year later when you asked me the same thing again. I still couldn't think of anything awful. And surely I would remember it. I fetched out your school reports from the bottom drawer of the desk. You were described as happy and enthusiastic at school.

Attentive and a very good pupil. You peruse them briefly. I forgot to ask what is making you question your childhood. Why didn't I? I presumed it was a nightmare. You have to leave to catch the train to London. For the second time, the subject of childhood trauma slips away.

You asked me the same thing on two other occasions. We got nowhere. But this time it's different. Why has this come up now I wonder? You say you are going to a weekly meditation group. Perhaps the meditating is stirring buried memories.

I'm confused and my mind is whirling. Did a friend really come to the house and harm you? I think through the friends who used to come and visit us. But surely if something awful had taken place, I would have known about it. I mean, you would have been upset, wouldn't you? This doesn't make any sense. We never left you alone in the house. One of us would have been there. Did I miss something? Oh no! The thought fills me with guilt. I mean, parents are supposed to protect their children. What sort of mother does this make me? A pretty useless one, that's what!

The next morning, we go out for breakfast. The weather's changed. It's blustery and the wind blows us along the beach, whipping at our backs. The clouds are dark and gathering for rain. I kick the sand, indignant and furious at the thought that someone may have harmed you. An innocent child does not deserve that. I hear of it happening all too often. You are quiet, your head is lowered, and your hands are thrust down in your pockets. I want to put my arm through yours, but I don't, because the last time I did this you pulled away. Sand sprays in my face and I like the feel of it, as well as the wind and the scudding, black clouds. The weather matches my mood. When we reach the café, it starts raining, and I find the sound of it tapping at the windows comforting. The waitress is nice and she smiles a lot. That helps. We came here once before. It's pleasant because there's nothing fancy about it. You get a good breakfast, with or without bacon, and a steaming mug of tea or coffee.

You look a little better today, less sort of nervous than yesterday, and you have a bit of colour in your cheeks. You bring over a paper from the stand and browse through the pages of yesterday's news. You are not working, as you have gone on sick leave, so what will you do with yourself? I pay the bill and thank our waitress and you leave a tip for her in the saucer.

We almost run down the rickety wooden steps to the beach. I like it when you go ahead as it means you feel brighter. Tiny waves of frothy seawater rush in around our shoes and we retreat, squealing like children. I'm not happy with the idea of you being here on your own and so far away.

'Come and stay awhile, Jasmine. You might even consider leaving your flat…' You reflect for a few moments, and yes, the idea appeals. The light is back in your eyes. You will give your landlord a month's notice. Good, that will give you time to sort through your belongings and it will also give you something practical to focus on.

You have money left over from teaching English in the holidays, so you buy yourself a second-hand car. It's old and not very big, but you reckon you can squeeze your belongings into it. One month later, almost to the day, you arrive at the spot where we have arranged to meet. It's a wild, blustery night in mid-November. You've had very little driving experience, so I am relieved to see you. Your car is piled high with your things. You roll down the window and grin, looking pleased with yourself. You've done really well.

Thank goodness I decided to buy the house. It was the south-facing garden that clinched the sale. The previous occupants were clearly not gardeners as there isn't a flower in sight. What it does mean is that the garden has a lot of potential. It will make a perfect project come the spring.

Muppet is happy to see you. He follows you down to your room and curls up on the sheepskin rug by your bed.

Love,

Mum

My dear Jasmine,

I'm not sure whether to get up or not. This is a funny in-between time. When you left Bournemouth, I contacted your father to inform him what was going on. Naturally, I told him about the awful memories that had surfaced, and the fact that you think a man who may have been a friend of ours behaved inappropriately. If he was surprised, he didn't express it, though he did go quiet. He said he would think about it, and if he had any thoughts, he would get back to me. He never did. Once again I found myself on my own.

The winter in which you came to stay seemed endless. January was cold but at least the days were getting longer. You settled in well. Muppet spent quite a bit of time with you and you liked that. I was glad to see you sketching and you said you were also keeping a journal. You've done that for years.

When signs of spring appear, my spirits lift. The woods are full of garlic leaves nudging their way through damp, fallen leaves, bracken and fern. In a couple of months, the flowers will open, and the scent of garlic will be at its height. I'm looking forward to that. We enjoy picking garlic leaves. I chop up the leaves and make soup with potatoes, onions and a few carrots. It was very tasty, wasn't it? You were thrilled when I found a recipe for wild garlic pesto, though we'll need about three or four bags of leaves to make a decent amount. I have a jar of raspberry vinegar in the cupboard so we can add that, as the recipe suggests adding some sweet vinegar. When you joked about starting up a pesto-making business, I think you were half serious, until you realised how many garlic leaves would be needed!

It was a great idea to volunteer at the school for young people with learning disabilities. You go every Thursday. Mucking out the horses is your favourite. Ever since you were a child, you've loved being with horses. I can still picture your face when we gave you a present of riding lessons for your tenth birthday. You also enjoy working in the gardens growing vegetables. At the end of the day, you always come home with a large bag of organic vegetables and a glow in your cheeks. The food tastes wonderful.

Hooray! You begin working in my garden, although I always think of it as ours. I suggest some curved flower beds because straight lines would be too rigid, and we begin planning the shapes. The next day, you fetch a spade out of the shed and set to work digging. Your enthusiasm is contagious and your energy limitless, like those huge skies in the east where there is more sky than land. The soil is full of stones so it's quite hard work. I add compost and start planting flowers. Your body seems very strong.

Your ideas keep coming. You have your eye on the piece of wasteland at the back of the house. It's a leftover area that is unsuitable for building as it has only one entrance. It will make an ideal vegetable garden. A friend comes over and puts a gate in the fence, so now we have direct access to the wasteland. I don't think you realised what hard work it would be. It takes almost ten days to clear the arching brambles, nettles and jagged stones. When you begin getting tired I take over from you. I'm glad to see you resting on the grass. Muppet stretches out beside you. After a while, you fetch out your guitar. And all the while, a cancer is growing in your breast. If only we had known about it sooner. I keep thinking about that. I must stop these thoughts as they are not getting me anywhere.

I have bags of compost to add to the wasteland soil and you help me carry them in from the car. When I make a joke about your strong arm muscles, you roll up your sleeve and clench your arm muscles to prove it! It's exciting because we are ready to plant. In no time we have a few rows of potatoes, some onions, a line of carrots and some cabbages. You seem to be thriving. I feel sure that being outside in the gardens and looking after the animals at the school is helping you more than anything.

We love going to the tip and behave like a couple of kids when we are there. There's something very satisfying about reclaiming an item and putting it to good use again. One week you find a pink bike and all it needs is a new tyre. I reckon Simon has a bit of a crush on you, because he is only too happy to clamber into a skip and fetch out some piece of timber for you. He is also putting aside a few larger pieces of wood for you, as you want to start making artwork for the garden.

My favourite is the one you did of butterflies hovering in long grass. You paint another one, with different colours, for Emma and Charlie. And I very much like the picture of the stork standing on one long, thin leg beside some water. You varnish them all to ensure they don't spoil if it rains. How they brighten up the corners of the garden!

During the ten months of your stay, we have only one major blip; however, it's a whopper. It was around the time you begin having counselling. You find a counsellor to work with and decide you will go on a weekly basis. But something happens in the fourth, or was it the fifth, session. Normally, you come home in a good mood, but this time you were in a very agitated state. You could hardly sit still and you didn't want to talk about it. The atmosphere in the house was like a bomb about to explode. I don't know whether I'm relieved or apprehensive when you tell me you are ready to talk now. It's probably a bit of both. You sit down on one sofa and I sit on the other. Clearly, you are nervous. I'm really not looking forward to this.

'Mum, how come you didn't protect me from the man who harmed me? It was your job to keep me safe.'

You poor darling, I'm surprised you haven't thought about this before. I suppose it came up in the counselling. I can't answer your question because I don't know why. It's a complete mystery to me. I feel ashamed of the fact that I didn't keep you safe. My head begins throbbing. Where are my words? I can usually find words. Not this time, though; they're jammed tightly in my throat. I wait for this to ease.

'I don't know, my love. I don't understand it myself. Perhaps he told you it was to be kept a secret just between the two of you. I believe that's what usually happens.'

You aren't very happy with that, but it's the best I can do. You look disappointed and then turn away. Something subtle changed in that moment. Is it safe to put your trust in me? Is that what you are thinking?

We don't resolve the matter but it sort of calms. What about your father? Where was he when it happened? You decide to bring the counselling to an end. I rather wish it had never begun.

In spite of our BLIP, we get back to gardening and taking Muppet out for walks. You are definitely less anxious and are even talking of finding a flat of your own. Living in a busy city no longer appeals and I am delighted when you decide to look for a place nearby.

It doesn't matter how old the child is when he or she leaves home; the sense of loss can be huge. People refer to it as the "empty nest syndrome". I don't much care for this term, as the word "syndrome" makes it sound like a medical condition, instead of an ending that brings a sense of loss. Emma was the first to leave and then you. So this will be the second time you leave home. Your bedroom is empty and the house rattles. Muppet misses you and mopes around the house looking for you, and wanders into the garden thinking you might be there. It takes him ages to settle. It's not just humans that feel like this, it's dogs too. Life is full of endings.

You are pleased when you find an art class near you. You are getting busy now because you have started up your own gardening business. *Soulful Gardening* is the name you give it. I feel very proud of you. See, I still have one of your business cards in my purse.

Love,

Mum

Sweetheart,

We had such a lovely Christmas, didn't we? I'm glad your friend enjoyed it too. She was clearly chuffed with the scarf and the fact that it is the same colour as her jumper. She asks me if I am psychic, which makes me laugh because I think I am! It is lovely seeing your expressions as you open my gifts. None of them are expensive yet each one is perfect. You want to wear the pyjamas, though you decide you can wait until bedtime. You finger a parcel, trying to work out what it contains, and then tear the paper off and toss it to one side. There is some natural shampoo made from extracts of jasmine (what other flower is there?), a pair of warm tights, a sketch pad with a hard cover, some pastel paints and a few other little things. Thank you for the pretty vase. I shall always keep the homemade book marker. I love how you've decorated it with beading.

Muppet was longing for a walk so I leave you both chatting and take him out. The sun is shining and I need the air. I begin to cry and feel better afterwards. The tension in my body has been building. I shall get back to yoga in the New Year, as the breathing helps to free my lungs. Do you ever cry, Jasmine? You are getting tired more easily now. I'm so sad. Actually, it's way beyond sad. This is unbearable. I must keep walking. The snow is melting. I love wearing wellies. It was because of all the snow that we decided to spend Christmas at home. I'm so glad we did.

I get back and prepare the Christmas meal for the three of us. I love hearing you both chattering next door. I can't remember when I last heard you this animated. I take out the glasses, warm the mulled wine and then pour it out. The spices smell great. The phone rings and it is Emma wishing us a Happy Christmas. They haven't opened their presents from us yet. Charlie speaks next and then Josh and Penny sing "We Wish You a Merry Christmas". They want to talk to you, so I leave you to it and go back to the kitchen. The radio is playing silly Christmas songs. I can't find any carols so switch it off. The parsnips, potatoes and leeks need another half-hour. The trout looks great. In they go. I've set the table with, of course, the usual crackers! There is a small Norwegian spruce tree in the corner, as you love the lights.

I wonder what this New Year will bring. We have another appointment with the healer in January. Let's hope he is helping you. I think you have two more injections of mistletoe to go. Charlie says he is booking a large cottage so we can all have a week away together. He is proposing the February half-term week and has asked where we'd like to go. I suggested somewhere in Dorset. I'll run that by you. I'm so looking forward to it.

Love,

Mum

Darling,

I'm awake early and am drinking tea in bed. I don't feel like getting up as it's still dark outside. How I miss being with you and Emma, Charlie, Josh and Penny. You were so pleased with your bedroom and it was the prettiest one by far. The double bed is super large and the cream covers are edged in lace. There are great views over the walled garden and look, you can see the hills in the distance. However, you are really tired after the journey and retire to bed early.

The next three days are scary. There is no sign of you the next morning. At first, I'm not too bothered, but when you don't get up in the evening for supper, I become more concerned. Emma and I take turns bringing you hot drinks all day. Each time I go in, I remove the old cup and replace it with another. I know you can hear me but you stay under the bedclothes without saying a word. Your clothes are piled on the chair beside the door and your red, woolly socks are on the top. Your old suitcase is on the floor with the lid flopped open, but apart from that, the room looks unbearably tidy and unlived in. We hear you going to the loo.

You don't get up the next day either. I go down to Emma's bedroom and find her sitting on the bed attempting to read a book. We hug each other tightly, each of us wondering if you are dying, but not daring to say so aloud.

On the third evening, we gather in the kitchen, uncertain what to do. We are all anxious. Charlie begins chopping vegetables. I can hear him now, slicing onions, peeling and cutting up carrots and cauliflower. He says he is making a vegetable soup. Emma and I take the soup up to your room and sit in the two little armchairs in the bay window. Please eat, Jasmine. You stir and slowly emerge from the bedclothes, then prop yourself up against the pillows and begin eating the soup. I can hardly contain myself. You don't want to talk, so Emma and I leave you and go downstairs.

In the morning, you come down to the kitchen. You are wearing jeans with a grey sweatshirt. The colour highlights your pallor. We try not to fuss over you too much, but it's wonderful to have you with us at the table. You ask for toast and marmalade. Josh and Penny have been worried about you. Whatever must they be thinking? This is a lot for them to take in. They know their young aunt has cancer... they sit either side of you, happy to have you back. After breakfast, you ask me if I will take you for a drive. I want to shout with joy. Of course I will! We leave the others to clear away and set off for the beach. You don't mind which beach we go to so I choose one with easy parking access. You are well wrapped up and have your favourite scarf looped around two or three times. Although it's a little chilly, we sit on the soft, grainy sand, our faces turned towards the faint warmth of the sun. You put a hand up to shield your eyes. Gulls shriek and squabble over pieces of bread, and waves with little white crests flop on the shore making swooshing sounds. Neither of us feel a need to talk. Sitting beside you on the beach feels nothing short of a miracle.

You ease yourself up and brush the sand from your coat. We begin slowly making our way towards the harbour, as we are meeting the others for lunch. I slow my pace to match yours. The wind is picking up and you adjust the scarf and wrap it around your ears. The harbour is packed with boats of all sizes and since there is little protection from the wind they are bucking and bobbing on the water, their masts clanking. I like the wildness of it. We have arranged to meet in a pub tucked around a corner. We are now out of the wind, and with the sun shining, it even feels warm. It's Valentine's Day. Normally, I don't make a fuss of it, but this one is different. I spot some large, chocolate hearts wrapped in red, shiny paper in a shop window, and buy one for each of us. Josh and Penny are delighted with theirs. Charlie is wearing a dark brown jacket and sits reading the papers. He tells me the local beer is good and I have a half pint. You order a glass of orange juice. Emma is taking some photos and Charlie then takes one of you, me and Emma. You are smiling and leaning towards me. The three of us are so happy together. I will never forget that.

Emma proposes a little fish restaurant for lunch. There is a lovely atmosphere inside. The owner gives us a warm welcome and moves two tables together. Each table is covered with a blue and white checked cloth which you say reminds you of cafés in France. We all decide to have the local fish of the day. Josh and Penny order lemonade and our beer comes in bottles. I am about to ask for a glass when Josh and Penny tell me it is much cooler to drink from the bottle. So I do, unsure whether they are impressed or not. Josh begins teasing me. I always know when he's about to because he grins and I can see him deciding on the joke he is about to tell me.

At the age of three, Josh was diagnosed with autism. Emma was beside herself with sadness. Little by little, the family adapt to the news. Josh is very sensitive and also bright in an unconventional way. Music fills his world, and his sense of rhythm and timing is second to none. Emma finds an excellent special school for him and life with autism begins to unfold.

You and Josh really understand each other, and when you hug him, he doesn't pull away like he does with other people. You somehow manage to land beside him in his world of autism. Josh is joking again. I probably fancy the waiter, he tells me, and I must say, he is very good-looking! Penny joins in the banter. We are in no hurry to leave. I'm unused to laughing so much. Life feels normal again. You are relaxed and we are all happy being together.

The following evening, you take us all to the local pub. Emma and I order a gin and tonic. We go back and prepare supper together and you set the table. Afterwards, we watch a silly television programme and you stay up late with us. I don't want the week to end. I'm not looking forward to the drive back and, although it's only three hours, it may be too long for you. I needn't have worried as you are fine. I feel sad to be dropping you back to your flat. I carry your suitcase and we go in together to warm the place up. I have a host of lovely memories of those few days. What I remember above all is how much stronger I felt when we were all together.

I'm sending you a hug. It's a bit of a grey old day out there. I'll phone you later, even though you probably won't answer. The light is coming back so at least the days are getting longer.

Love,

Mum

Jasmine, my love,

What a tough day it's been. I'm exhausted but I won't to go to bed yet as I know I shan't sleep. Was it really only this morning when you phoned?

'Please will you take me to the local hospital? My breathing isn't right and I think I might have fluid on my lung.' I remember every word. My body chills. Bloody hell, this is not good. I can't find the energy to be remotely cheerful in the car. You are the same, so we drive to the hospital in silence. I'm glad we don't have far to go. Unlike the large hospital, we don't have to wait long before being seen. I put a coin in the drinks machine and press the button for white coffee. It isn't strong enough, maybe nothing would be. You don't want anything. You ask me to come with you when your name is called. Of course I will. I want to hear every word the doctor says. He isn't wearing a white coat, which makes it feel a bit more relaxed. He has a beard and I would guess he is in his early forties. I find myself wondering if he has children. Your notes are open on the desk. He glances down at them then takes out his stethoscope and says he would like to listen to your chest. I watch him listening, first at the front and then at the back, then he sits down stroking his beard. How grave he looks. My stomach tightens. He says he will send you for a chest X-ray, as this will show us what is going on. Do I want to know? You don't flinch or say anything. Your face gives nothing away, you poor darling.

Afterwards we sit in a long corridor to wait. A young family sits next to us. The mother holds a sleeping baby in her arms, a toddler runs up and down the passage and a third child is egging her on. The toddler reminds me of you at that age with her mass of riotous, golden curls and deep-set, blue grey eyes. On hearing all the commotion, a nurse in a white uniform comes out and tells us that we won't have too long to wait.

The same doctor sees us, but we are in a different room. Your X-rays are clipped to a screen and when he switches the light on it blinks a few times. He opens your brown folder, then looks up at the screen for what seems like ages. This is unbearable. Then he turns to face you.

'It's not good news,' he says. 'I'm afraid you have a real battle on your hands.'

Why is the word *battle* used so often? Does he think you are not trying hard enough? He obviously knows you are not having chemotherapy, but it doesn't mean you don't want to get well. That's what I'd like to say to him, but of course I don't. You don't say anything either. He then tells us that your cancer has spread to your lung. He will refer you to the main hospital to have your lung drained. My head spins. Like zombies, we get up and walk out of the room. I can't find the car keys. They are in my bag of course. It's so grey outside.

No wonder you can't breathe properly. God, this is grim news. I don't know what to do or what to say to you. There are no words. This is such a jolt, especially after the last session of healing when you said that the lump in your breast had got smaller. My spirits lifted, but that's all been wiped out now. You ask me to take you back to your flat. It is unbearably hard dropping you at your door. 'Would you like to come and stay for a bit?' You shake your head and tell me you want to manage. Then you close your front door and I sit motionless in the car.

You say so little. And you rarely answer your phone, so I never know when might be a good time to call. Maybe there isn't one. You are retreating into yourself and I can't reach you there.

Love,
Mum

My love,

What a joy to see you this morning. My timing is good as you are just back from your art class. The painting is still wet so you have it propped against the radiator. It's gorgeous… The sky is dazzling in shades of yellow and orange, and makes a perfect contrast with the blue and green hills and turquoise sea. It is beautiful. I step back to look at it from a distance and notice the shape of a dolphin, its underbelly curving beneath the sea. You are thrilled to see the dolphin as you hadn't planned it. You have had an affinity with dolphins and whales for as long as I can remember. Your eyes are shining and you laugh and tuck your hair away behind an ear.

'I'm thinking of having an exhibition of my artwork in town.'

'What a great idea! Will you have an open evening?' We are getting quite carried away with ourselves.

'Oh yes. We'll have sparkling wine and canapés.' This is so nice. We are a team again. You aren't pushing me away as you have done on numerous occasions.

Imagine that, Jasmine. I forgot about your cancer this morning. I didn't think that was possible. We are going back to the hospital in a couple of days for your lung to be drained. Emma will join us there.

Love,

Mum

10th April, 2013, 2am

Sweetheart,

You were right. There was fluid on your lung. The procedure to drain it isn't at all comfortable but your breathing is much improved afterwards. Oh my love, you seem so accepting of it all, but I don't suppose that you are for one minute. What happens to the fluid now? I can't imagine that it will simply go away.

You have some good days, and then days with less energy, so you rest in the afternoons. I never know how you are because you rarely answer your phone or respond to text messages. It's maddening and it makes me anxious. The mistletoe injections have finished, though you are continuing with the acupuncture.

Hilary is coming over tomorrow. I've made some soup. I am beyond sad. I almost don't know how I feel. I don't have to make an effort to be upbeat or anything else with her. 'Stay positive,' someone said only a few days ago. I could have thumped her. There is nothing positive happening. It's a mess, pure and simple, and my daughter is only thirty-eight. I wish this was me and not you, Jasmine. I'm old enough to go, but you're not.

My mind is buzzing. No wonder I can't sleep. For some reason I keep thinking about your birth. Did you somehow sense as a baby that life wasn't going to be easy? I ask that because I was well on the way to giving birth to you when the labour pains suddenly stopped. It was as if you'd changed your mind. The midwife tried to reassure me but I was scared. You didn't stir again for several hours. Mind you, when the labour pains recommenced, you wasted no time forging your way into the world. The midwife wrapped you in a soft blanket, then placed you in my arms telling me it's all been worth it. The pain and loneliness of the night dissolved and I wanted to cry with the beauty of you. You were so tiny. I stroked your light, downy hair, marvelling at its softness, and drew you close. I remember the smell of you. Your little hand curled around my finger and you scrunched up your face, and for a brief moment, opened your eyes and gazed ahead. Your eyes were a most unusual shade of grey blue. Giving birth is a miracle. I felt such a rush of love. It was the same feeling as three years earlier when I first held Emma in my arms. You have made us into a family of four.

I want to sleep, but I can't. I put the kettle on and get out some photo albums. Why am I putting myself through this? They are unbearable. I get no further than the second page. How does such a beautiful baby, who looks so content and full of life, grow up and become so ill?

Love,

Mum

Dear Jasmine,

From the age of eight or nine, you became concerned about dying. It was triggered by the death of our cat, who was run over on the main road. You were really upset when the driver didn't stop. I explained to you that a car doesn't have to stop for a cat, though it does for a dog, and you thought this very unfair. You found a shoebox and lined it with newspaper and, although her body was cold, you placed one of your dolls' blankets over her to try to keep her warm. My mother, who knitted all your dolls' blankets, promised to knit you another one. Then we buried her in a corner of the garden. For days afterwards, you thought you could hear her miaowing. You asked me to dig her up because you were worried she was trying to get out of the box. I managed to persuade you that she was dead and that she wouldn't come back to life again.

'But how will she feed herself now she is dead?'

Some three or four weeks later, your thoughts went a step further.

'What will it be like when I am buried in the ground? How will I eat my Weetabix cereal for breakfast and play with my favourite Cindy doll?'

The death of our little cat had really started something. I explained that you wouldn't need any food when you die, and gave you some reasons, though I can't for the life of me remember what they were.

Your big question came some ten years later. My father had recently died and we were on our way to his funeral. You leaned forwards from the back of the car.

'What exactly happens when we die?'

Goodness, what a question, though I guess it was the perfect time to ask about dying. We didn't have long until we arrived at the church, but I made a start. This is how I understand it, Jasmine. I told you that it is only the body that dies, and that we all have a soul. When the body dies, the soul leaves the body and crosses over to the other side. Our soul never dies.

Love,

Mum

Dear Jasmine,

Emma has told Josh and Penny that you are not getting better. I really feel for them. You know how much they love you. They want to come and stay so they can see you for themselves. You arrange a weekend and I lend you some extra bedding. You have such a lovely time together, painting and cooking. Josh makes a bit of a joke about your lentil burgers, though Penny is a bit more diplomatic. On Sunday, the four of us meet for tea and cakes at a café within walking distance of your flat. You insist on paying, and when you walk over to the till, I see how rounded your shoulders and back are. You are literally swelling up with fluid. Had I not known it was you, I would have thought you an old lady. How wretched you look. I brush away my tears and drive you back to your flat.

Are we being too brave, Jasmine? We never cry together. I do that on my own. I wonder if you do too. Do you know how unwell you are? Your way is not to talk, but it isn't mine.

We take you back to hospital to have your lung drained. This time, they drain off seven litres of fluid. I mean, how on earth can a lung hold so much? The doctor is going to plug the lining of the lung with a substance that will hopefully prevent the fluid from getting in. But where will it go instead? Surely it has to go somewhere? Are we just buying time? I haven't spoken with a doctor so I've no idea. No one says anything. You are disappearing before my eyes. I'm losing you.

I begin counting the weeks. Four weeks pass, then five… but we don't get to six. The fluid surges back with the zeal of a tidal wave. In the end, there is so much sloshing around it is a wonder you don't burst open. After the lung is drained, the doctor leaves the tube *in situ*. Now any fluid will drain directly into a bag and a district nurse will call twice a week to empty it. Oxygen is helping you breathe more easily, so two large cylinders will be delivered to your flat. And all the while you say nothing.

You still want to manage in your flat. I doubt you will change your mind. It was like this when you were a child.

Do you remember the Easter holiday when we rented a cottage for a week? One of the walks proved a bit long, to say the least, and the only way back to the car was up a steep hill. I must say, it looked a bit daunting, even to me. You stopped in your tracks and told us that you couldn't, and wouldn't, go a step further. You were so tired. The problem was that the sun was going down and it would be dark within the hour. So I began to tell you a story. Little Red Riding Hood was your favourite. Two little sisters, much the same ages as you and Emma, were on their way back to the woods. The big, bad wolf was out on the prowl looking for little or big humans. He soon got the scent of the girls. Hiding behind a tree, he waited to pounce on them… By now you were completely absorbed in the tale. You took hold of my hand and we began climbing the hill. Emma was the first to spot our car in the car park below and you both ran down the slope in a bid to get there first. That evening in the pub, we dined out on sausages, chips, Coke – all the things we had bribed you with! Your dad got out a map and showed you how far you had walked, and you both beamed with pride.

Are you preparing for bed or maybe you are there already. How much longer can you manage in your flat? I am trying not to think about it. It is literally a day at a time. I've made a large pot of dahl and will bring half of it over tomorrow. I've used all kinds of spices, though it won't be overwhelmingly hot. I think you will enjoy it.

'Night night, treasure.'

Love,

Mum

Sweetheart,

Emma has invited you to stay for two weeks. It comes at a perfect time and you accept their invitation. I sense you are pleased to be going. I drive you halfway and Emma meets us and takes you back with her. I know they will take such good care of you. Although I haven't gone away anywhere, it feels a bit like being on holiday. Only now do I realise how much I worry about you, particularly as you live on your own.

Some of the flowers we planted are coming up, and the garden is full of foxgloves. The wisteria is doing well and it won't be long before the purple tendrils appear. I've planted a shrub of jasmine, your favourite flower (of course!). I've put it in the far corner. It will have a lovely smell and when it gets bushy I will trail it along the fence. And that stub of a rose bush you gave me is thriving. You always said it would. It seems ages ago since we began creating the garden, though it's no time really. I'm rather hoping that the pond you made will attract dragonflies and other wildlife. That was always your intention for having one.

The hardest part for you was digging the hole, as the soil was sticky and bound with clay and stones. You were undeterred and three days later the hole is deep enough and wide enough for a pond. I have a great photo of you standing in it. Although tired, you are clearly proud of your work. Finally, you ensure the bottom of the hole is level before lining it with black plastic sheeting. You already have some flat stones to fit around the edges and conceal the lining. The moment has arrived. It's time to fill the pond with water.

First thing in the morning, you go out to check the level of the water. It's the same as when you left it, so it's not leaking. You are thrilled. By way of celebrating, you go out to buy a fish and come back carrying a goldfish swimming in a plastic bag of water. You name her Goldie. As the sun sets behind the poplar trees, we ceremoniously tip Goldie out of her plastic bag into the spacious waters of her new home.

After you moved into your own flat, I went out to buy a mate for Goldie, though I rather think it was me who was in need of a mate. The new fish was not nearly as robust as Goldie, and three days later I find her body floating on the surface of the water. I remove her and bury her amongst the flowers, surprised at how upset I am.

After making the pond, you decide to make herb and vegetable boxes. How you love making things. You already have some longer pieces of wood, so all you have to do is saw them into two different lengths. The first box is soon ready. My job is to line it, fill it with soil, and then plant it with peppermint and chives. The second box is slightly larger so I plant it with sage and rosemary, a few lettuces, and sow nasturtium seeds in the spaces. By the way, the herbs are all thriving. I'll bring you over some chives and mint. A robin has taken up residence in the garden. He wasn't here when you were staying. It hasn't rained in a while so he has his eye on the bird bath below.

I phoned Emma yesterday for an update. When she

goes out to work, a neighbour comes over to prepare lunch for you. I imagine she stays on for a bit of a chat. That's nice that you are not on your own. Emma and Charlie have some good friends in the village. When Josh and Penny get back from school, you apparently sit round the table cutting out fabrics together, transforming a cardboard box into something special. Charlie complains about the mess!

It won't be long before it's time to bring you back. I'm sure you will feel better for your stay with them. It is more sociable for you and it must be nice not having to think about shopping and cooking. I've made a few things for you to put in the fridge and will bring them over. I wonder how you are.

Love,

Mum

Dear Jasmine,

I don't know how much longer you can cope in your flat. I feel so helpless. Your energy is very up and down. Emma has just phoned. She says she is inviting you for another two-week stay, and they are converting the little downstairs sitting room into a bedroom so you don't have to go up and down the stairs. That's a good idea. I'll take you halfway and Emma will come and meet us like we did before.

Sleep tight.

Love,

Mum

Dear Jasmine,

You are with Emma and family. Charlie is apparently on nights, so it is Emma who prepares the meal in the evening. She tells me you rest during the day and are up and dressed by the time Josh and Penny get back from school. As before, the three of you sit round the table cutting out pieces of fabric; gluing, stitching and transforming something ordinary into a piece of beauty. You have shown Penny how to make a felt brooch and you encourage her to make one of her own.

In the evenings, you wrap yourself in Emma's green blanket and curl up on the sofa to watch television. Although you used to tease Emma about her appalling taste in Hollywood movies, I understand you are rather enjoying watching some of them! Freddie, their dog, jumps up and slides under the blanket next to you, and although not officially allowed there, he thinks that if he remains out of sight, no one will notice him. And I believe nobody has the heart to move him. I wish I was there watching television with you, but at least you are not on your own and are being well cared for.

When it's time for you to come home again, Emma and the children, along with Freddie, bring you to a halfway point. Here we are next to a canal. You sit at the table with Emma's green blanket wrapped around your shoulders. You look miserable. Your skin is a little greyer and your eyes lack lustre. You don't say a word. When Freddie jumps up beside you, you don't pat him or take any notice of him. I wonder if he followed you around in a bid to look after you like Muppet used to.

Some dogs can sense when a person is unwell and they endeavour to make them better simply by being with them. Muppet first did this with Margot when we stayed with her in France. There were seven or eight people staying in the house, but it was always Margot he followed. After chasing her cat over the wall, presumably to establish the garden as his territory, Muppet trotted behind Margot and followed her into the garden. When she sits down with a cup of coffee, he curls under her legs in a bid for the shade. In the evenings, we used to watch a little television, and Muppet was invariably curled up beside her on the rug. It is quite amusing because Margot doesn't particularly like dogs, though she does concede that her little shadow is really rather sweet.

Three months later, there is a phone call from a friend of Margot's to inform me that she has just been diagnosed with cancer. Even then I don't put two and two together. It slowly begins to dawn on me that Muppet was probably sensing this, and in his own way was trying to help her. I am pleased to say that four months later there was another phone call to tell me that Margot had been given the all-clear.

If I had put two and two together and realised that Muppet was following you around because he sensed you were unwell, we would have discovered your cancer at least a year sooner. Anyway, I've stopped blaming myself. It's just how it was. And everything is easier to make sense of in hindsight.

Emma and I leave you with the children and go for a

short walk along the towpath. We speak regularly on the phone so there isn't much more to add. We walk as far as a black canal boat with an upturned bike and a pot of plastic daffodils on its roof and then turn back.

You hardly say a word on the journey home. I take you back to your flat and we have a cup of tea together. What happens now? The nurse pops by twice a week to empty your bag. You see your GP as and when you need to, and two or three friends drop by, sometimes with homemade soup. The days pass slowly, and all the while you are getting weaker.

I feel so alone. It's a day at a time. There's not much sleep to be had tonight. Thinking of you, Jasmine.

Love,

Mum

Sweetheart,

In a couple of weeks, you are going back to Emma's. She has not put a timescale on this visit, so it remains open-ended. I'd like to do something special with you before you go. I am wondering if you might enjoy the family circus that is setting up on the common. People talk very highly of it. Let's see what you think. If you like the idea, I might invite a friend to join us, and maybe her son might come too. He is a bit younger than you.

Love,
Mum

Dear Jasmine,

You are slow to answer the door. It's not a good sign. Then you open the door just a fraction as if wondering who is there. You are not pleased to see me; quite the contrary. I follow you into the living room pretending everything is okay when clearly it isn't. Why do I do this? I've just collected five rather expensive circus tickets, and if we don't go, the others won't be able to either. Who gives a toss about the others? Apparently I do.

'Are you sure you want to go?' You don't reply, though you fetch your light jacket hanging in the hall. What has changed your mood? You said you were keen to go. We are both tense on arrival. The others are waiting for us and I introduce you to them, as it's the first time you have all met. We find seats on one of the benches near the back. The tent is filling up fast. The music strikes up and two clowns begin circling the floor, tickling the chins of excited children, most of whom seem to be near the front. You are quiet. Then a moment later, you stand up and announce quite loudly that you don't want to sit next to me. The others duly shuffle along to make a space for you. Oh no! I feel so hurt and embarrassed by your behaviour. Why don't I just get up and leave? I wish I had. But instead I stay rooted to the bench in that red and white striped tent. I hardly remember anything about that evening.

You will be leaving in a few days and I so wanted this to be special. We don't speak on the way home. I'm unable to make sense of what just triggered your behaviour. I feel bewildered but mad as well. Was the music too loud, the tent too busy, the bench too hard, or what? I don't want to say anything I might later regret, so we bid each other a rather curt goodnight. You get out of the car and put your key in the front door without looking back.

Two days later, your cousin Adrian drives you over to Emma's. He says you were very chatty all the way there.

Love,
Mum

Jasmine,

You've been gone a week. Your routine doesn't vary at Emma's. You rest during the day so that you will have some energy for when the children get home from school. It seems to be working well with you sleeping downstairs. You can wash and brush your teeth in the little cloakroom leading off the kitchen. It is wonderful knowing you are being well cared for. In a few days' time, you will be thirty-nine. I have a few little gifts I would like to bring over. I know the house is a bit crowded so I can always stay the night in a bed and breakfast. What do you think?

You tell Emma that you want to be a bit stronger before I visit, so it looks like I won't be seeing you on your birthday. Emma tries to persuade you to change your mind; however, I think we both know you are unlikely to shift on this. I can make no sense of it. Once again, we are back in the situation in which either Emma, or I, are in favour, though not both of us. This time, I am the one left outside in the cold. Emma tells you that you are being selfish, but still you don't change your mind. However, you send me a lovely text thanking me for the gifts. I feel heartbroken.

What would have happened if I had just driven over and handed you a huge bunch of flowers? I didn't want to take the chance because I couldn't bear the thought of being shunned by you. Now I will never know what the outcome might have been.

There is little point trying to persuade you to see me when your mind is made up. Emma knows it too. I recall the weekend I was working away and my parents came over to look after you both. I returned home early Sunday evening to find you still sitting at the kitchen table. In front of you was a plate with half a fish finger and a small amount of potato. Both were stone-cold. My mother had been insisting that you finish it before you can have ice cream. By now you couldn't care less about ice cream. My father stood by awkwardly, not knowing what to say or do, and Emma hovered in the background. Much to the relief of everyone, I made light of it, fetched your plate and scooped the remains into the bin. I don't who was the more stubborn, you or my mother. You and Emma left the room and I heard you giggling as you watched *Heidi*, your favourite programme of the week.

There was something distinct and almost laudable about how resolute you were as a child. You didn't think about the outcome. There was also that time when you locked yourself in the sitting refusing to come out. I can't for the life of me remember what prompted you to do that. Your father and I remained on the outside, trying to persuade you to unlock the door. The more we did this, the more fixed you became. In fact, you turned on the television and increased the volume. Your father was exasperated and raised his voice as he banged on the door. Nothing would make you budge. I don't remember how long you stayed there. It was only when you had assurances there would be no reprimand that you finally unlocked the door. You emerged as if nothing untoward had happened.

. Truth to tell, I think your father and I were impressed

by your tenacity, though of course we didn't admit it at the time.

Please, though, enough is enough. I really want to see you, Jasmine.

Love,

Mum

Jasmine, my love,

I've not seen you since you left. I would love to be there helping out. Emma is struggling to manage work as well as look after you and keep an eye on the children. Charlie is working late shifts. I've been away for a weekend to stay with a friend. We watched a film and for two whole hours I didn't think of you. There's no point being at home as you're not there. We're waiting, just waiting.

And then comes the phone call. It's Charlie. He tells me you were admitted to the hospice this morning. My stomach turns over and I almost stop breathing. Emma will phone later to tell me more.

You didn't have the strength to get out of bed. Oh, you poor darling. Emma hears you calling. I imagine she only has to look at you to assess the situation. She asks whether it may be time for you to have some extra care. You agree. The hospice apparently have a room. Emma gathers up a few of your personal things. I would have liked to have been there too. You want the blue woollen blanket that you find so comforting, some candles, your dream catcher and the little painting you did about a year ago of the dove flying through a ring of fire into the freedom of the skies.

I drive over the next day. From this point on, you turn away all visitors, except for Emma, Charlie and the children. I don't know what to do with myself. The chapel in the hospice provides a peaceful refuge. It even has a picture of a dove that is not too dissimilar to yours, except that the style is different and it's much bigger. There is also a huge stained glass window of St Francis of Assisi surrounded by birds and different animals, and even on a gloomy day it throws pretty patterns into the room. In the corner is a table with a pin board where we can write messages to our loved ones. Each time I am there, I write you a message. It's like sending you a little prayer. Today's is very simple – *I love you, Jasmine.*

My body feels numb. Maybe it's just as well, and my mind has more or less clouded over. I feel an outsider in every sense of the word. However, my visits with the chaplain are different because with him I come alive. I'm so glad he is there. He's Irish, Jasmine. His eyes are a deeper shade of blue than yours and they sparkle with so much joy. He has a bushy, brown beard and when he smiles, which is often, there is quite a gap between his front teeth. He is very kind and we usually go and talk in the chapel. He never seems to be in any hurry, and whenever I cry he doesn't try and cheer me up.

I have told him that I hope you will have another near-death experience like you did when you were only fifteen. Just like now, you were very ill. Your eating disorder began about a year after your father and I separated. You got thinner and thinner until finally pneumonia set in. I was relieved you were at last in hospital, because now you would have to accept treatment of some kind. But one night, you nearly died. The next day, you described what happened to your grandmother. Instead of dying, you lifted out of your body and found yourself in a tunnel of bright light. Your grandfather was there to welcome you, his arms outstretched. He told you that it was not your time to go yet, so you came back to us. I'd never heard of near-death experiences back then. Anyway, I am praying you will have another one, because as far as I can see, nothing else will save you.

To my surprise, the chaplain then proceeds to tell me about his own near-death experience. Ten years ago, his heart condition began to worsen and the doctor recommended surgery if he was to have any chance at all. The operation was more complicated than they had anticipated and the surgeon eventually gave up and pronounced the chaplain dead. His three sons were waiting in the corridor and they were called in. But just like you, instead of dying, the chaplain lifted out of his body, and when he looked back, he saw himself lying on the operating table with his sons around him. The chaplain was now surrounded by three tall, beautiful beings, each of whom emanated a tremendous sense of unconditional love. The intensity and beauty of their presence was so profound that all he wants is to go with them. But just like your grandfather, they tell him that it isn't his time to go. And so he returns to his body leaving the doctors mystified. He has somehow made a miraculous recovery.

The chaplain sits back in his chair and wipes away a tear. He smiles and tells me that there is only love beyond death. I am very happy that he is there keeping an eye on you. He visits you every day, Jasmine, even if it is only for five minutes. He says you are usually in bed with your back turned, and although you are too tired to speak, he senses you know he is there. He tells me how bright and intelligent your soul is and I feel so moved that he can see that.

About a week after your admission, the head nurse invites me in to have a talk with her. We go to the visitors' room. Emma comes too and there is another nurse present.

There are three large windows overlooking the garden, giving the room a feeling of light and space. The trees nearest the windows seem to loom like sleeping giants waiting for spring to arrive. The nurse is probably in her late fifties. She has curly grey hair, soft eyes, and a kind demeanour balancing an air of efficiency. She doesn't say much at first, but when she leans back in her chair and removes her glasses, I know she is about to tell me how you are. I shrink back as she informs me that you are dying, and then gives a timescale that turns out to be horribly accurate. Much to my relief, no one tries to fill the empty silence. Emma sits there quietly, her head bowed. She has already been given the news. The rain begins tapping on the windows and the nurse reaches over and passes me a box of tissues. She must have done that a hundred times.

My sadness fills the room. I can't take in what she has just told me. I suppose I don't want to because I'm not ready to let you go, not when there is still a chance you might have another near-death experience. This tiny glimmer of a possibility is all I had left to shield me from the terrifying prospect that your life is coming to an end and that mine will have to continue.

The nurses surely know that you don't want to see me. Whatever must they think? And then I realise I don't care, and anyway, they are probably well versed in all kinds of situations. All I have to do is keep going. I ask her if I might have time with you after you die, or earlier if you lose consciousness. 'Is that possible?' She nods.

'You can take as much time as you need.'

Emma is ready to go home, but I tell her I want to sit in the chapel, as I have much to digest. She nods. I go and breathe in the peace of the chapel. Moments later, a young woman follows me in and I watch her go over to the table to write a message. She turns and when she sees me she comes and sits near me. 'My husband is dying,' she tells me and our eyes meet.

'But we don't know what to say to each other, so I just sit in a chair beside him and hold his hand.' I nod in sympathy, aware of a stab of envy because at least she is at his side, holding his hand. I know it would be agony watching your young life ebb away, Jasmine, but I can't help feeling it would be a million times easier than being kept away like this.

'Please don't die, Jasmine.'

Part Two

Between Worlds

17th Nov, 2013, 5.30pm

Jasmine, my love,

Your father and I are meeting up this evening. It's been ages so I'm a little nervous about the prospect, though I imagine he is too. I expect we'll go to the pub and talk. I'll let you know how it goes.

Love,

Mum

Dear Jasmine,

I was quite taken aback when I saw your father outlined through the glass door. It was like being transported back all those years ago when we first met. What year was it...? Oh yes, it was 1969. I was in my second year of nursing in Oxford and Alan was about to graduate.

From the moment I first saw Oxford, I loved it, so much so that I chose to train as a nurse in order to live and work there. It doesn't sound a very solid reason to become a nurse now, does it? But that's how it was. Falling in love with your father wasn't quite like that. It was much slower. We met because he left his squash racquet in the house that we were now renting. He called back for it, and when I saw him outlined through the glass front door, I recognised him as one of the undergraduates who had just moved out.

'Sorry to bother you, but I left my squash racquet behind the door of my room. It's the one at the top of the house.'

Would you believe that this is also my room? He tells me his name is Alan. He's shy, broad-shouldered, and his eyes are the same colour as yours. The racquet is concealed under my coat and I hadn't even noticed it. He doesn't stay long, though in that time, I must have expressed my own interest in squash. Anyway, we end up playing together. In fact, we play most weeks after that. I give your father a run for his money, I can tell you, and from time to time I win, though he is none too gracious when I do. Three months later, he moves to London.

Although the games of squash come to an end, we begin writing to each other, of course it was letters in those days! Meeting in London is more difficult what with my shift duties. He is renting a room in a large house that's not nearly as nice as the one in Oxford, but that's London prices for you.

We don't talk about "going out with each other" in the way I've heard you and Emma refer to boyfriends. We are young and quite shy about such matters, which is strange when you think we met at the tail end of the "swinging" sixties, a time of revolutionary British pop music, fashion, protests against the American role in the war in Vietnam, hippies, peace and love.

After spending a second or third weekend with Alan, I get back and make an appointment to see my GP to ask her for oral contraception, as the condom isn't that reliable. Jasmine, in 1961, when the pill was first available, it was only given to married women. Can you believe that this didn't change until 1967? Anyway, I have to wait for the first day of my next period before I can start taking it. I can still see the purple packet on my bedside table.

But, you see, I'm already pregnant. Such a terrible shock! I'm dreading telling my parents. They are horrified, justifiably so, as I'm only twenty and have only known Alan for six months. My mother suggests we run away to Gretna Green and pretend we have been married longer, anything to avoid the scandal of a child being born out of wedlock. When I mention possibly terminating the pregnancy, my father has something to say on the matter.

'You never know, this may be your only pregnancy, so I think you should keep your baby.' You know how quiet your grandfather is. He really surprises me sometimes. By now,

I'm so confused I don't know what to do. A friend of Alan's knows someone in Bristol who recently had an abortion and he drives us to meet her. She rather enjoys regaling us with her tale of woe. What with the conversation and the heat of the dingy pub, I feel sick and get up to leave. Alan follows. By now, I know I will not terminate my pregnancy but I don't say a word to Alan. We drive back to Oxford wrapped in the silence of our thoughts, my head aching from the tension of it all. His friend drives off and we stand outside my house, not quite knowing what to say. Then out of the blue, Alan tells me that I don't have to have an abortion.

'We could get married instead.'

Jasmine, your father's proposal wasn't in the least bit romantic. There was definitely no prince on a white horse preparing to whisk me away to his castle! And now that I think about it, there was no mention of love either, but somehow getting married felt right. I don't know how long we stood there before I reached for his hand.

My parents didn't take to Alan. His hair was too long for their middle-class notions of respectability, and when they discovered that he was a Sociology graduate, well, that was the end of something that never really got started.

Jasmine, I'm sorry you haven't seen him for a while, because there was quite a strong bond between you both. I thought we had a strong bond too. Maybe that's why you can't see me now. I've no idea. I would like to think it was that. This is a nightmare.

Love,
Mum

Dear Jasmine,

It wasn't easy seeing your dad, far from it, and I'm glad it's over. He looks much the same except that he has gained weight.

We get to the pub early so it is almost empty. The woman at the bar is so preoccupied with wiping it down that at first she doesn't see us. Alan buys the drinks. I order a double brandy. We go over to the far corner of the room and sink into two leather armchairs. Although there's a fireplace, it's a bit dreary, because instead of logs burning in the grate there's a rather nondescript basket of dried flowers. The brandy helps to ease my sense of wretchedness. Alan is rummaging through his pockets, and he pulls out a scrunched-up piece of paper with an estimate of the cost of a funeral. I can't believe this. Are we here to discuss the cost of a funeral, your funeral? You are still alive. This is your nineteenth day in the hospice. I begin to cry and Alan doesn't know what to do. He says he is going to Canada in a week's time. So bloody what! For a while I can't speak.

Okay, so maybe we might have a little conversation about arrangements. I'm so sorry, Jasmine. Alan asks if I will pay half the costs. This is getting worse. Of course I will! I cry again. Is this what we have come to? Please forgive me for telling you this when you are still alive. It must sound dreadful. The conversation stops and starts. By now, I've lost all hope. I tell your father that if you die, I would like my friend Hilary to hold your service. She is a minister, though what is much more important is that she loves you and knows you well. She will make the service very personal for us as a family. Alan nods. I wasn't expecting him to agree.

It was hard getting to sleep that night, but I must have dropped off because I dreamt about you. It was one of those vivid dreams so I don't have to write it down to remember it. You enter my room wearing a long, white nightgown, which is unusual, as you much prefer pyjamas, then you sit on the end of my bed, your hair loose around your shoulders. Your face is sad and beautiful. You tell me you have come to talk to me. 'Mum, I'm scared and I feel very lonely, but you have to let me go. I am not going to get well.'

My sobbing wakes the children and brings Emma into the room. I tell her how lonely you are and she says she will phone the hospice. It doesn't have to be like this. I could be there with you now. You don't have to be alone. I wouldn't say a word if you didn't want me to, not a word.

First thing in the morning, Emma suggests I invite a friend over to spend the day with me. She's right. I'm on my own too much. She probably thinks I am losing the plot. Maybe I am. I tell her I'd like my brother to come over. He drops everything and says he'll be with me just before lunchtime. How kind. It's a long drive for him. His presence calms me and we have a nice walk around the reservoir. Like dad, his humour is dry and he even makes me laugh. I buy us sandwiches in a pub and he has a pint of beer. That night, we put a single mattress for him at the foot of my bed. I feel safe with him there and sleep better than I have for ages.

Tomorrow, I have an appointment with the chaplain,

which I'm looking forward to. I'm thinking of you as ever, sweetheart. Thank you for coming to visit me in a dream.

Love,

Mum

Sweetheart,

Does everyone think their marriage will last forever? I have to say that I did, though after sixteen years it begins crumbling. We try some counselling and stagger on for another four years. However, we are unable to sort it out and finally we mutually agree to part. I'm so sorry. It was so hard for you and Emma. There are more conscious ways to end a marriage, of bringing it to a close, thanking each other for the children and the good times. However, we didn't know how to do that.

Emma goes away to college, removing herself from the situation. However, this leaves you on your own at a time when your home is tumbling around your ears. I'm not sure we fully appreciate the impact this has on children. You were upset and angry, though the anger remains unexpressed. Instead, it turns inwards and begins eating away at you. You begin losing weight and then you lose a bit more. You end up in hospital for three weeks. You were also referred to a psychologist. You like her enormously. She suggests you write down all your feelings and then share them with her the following week. What a dark and lonely time. Your recovery is slow but sure. And twenty years later, here we are again. You are back, not in a hospital, but in a hospice.

Do you know, Jasmine, when I began writing to you, I thought about addressing you as Katherine, the name we gave you at birth. About seven or eight years ago you asked us to start calling you Jasmine. I was surprised and also puzzled, because you gave us no reason why, or how, you came by the new name Jasmine. I had to keep practising saying your new name aloud, in order to get used to it. And some three years later when I accidentally called you Katherine, you were furious, though you softened when I told you that I'm doing my best. You left Katherine behind a number of years ago. And now I am using the name of your choice and not ours.

I'm looking forward to my appointment with the chaplain in the morning. I don't know how I would manage without him. He tells me you are very sensitive to noise and that even a little knock on your door disturbs you. You are in a very deep place. I can't help you. I know now that you are dying and I've let go of all hope that you will have another near-death experience. I feel wretchedly resigned and send you so much love... I can't write anymore.

Love,

Mum

Treasure,

I thought you might slip into unconsciousness as I've seen others do, in which case I would sit with you for however many hours or days were left to you. But in the end it isn't anything like that.

The children are in bed, so it must be about eight o'clock in the evening when the phone rings. I hurry to answer it. Emma sounds very scared. 'Come quickly, Mum.' No sooner do I put the phone down than it rings again. This time, it's a nurse telling me you are in your dying phase. I slam the receiver down before she can finish and run out of the house into the darkness. My heart is beating so fast I think my chest might explode. What on earth am I to do? Charlie is at work and I have to get to the hospice, but I can't leave Josh and Penny alone. A neighbour is hurrying towards the house. Emma has obviously phoned her. Her husband will drive me, she says. I am so shaky this is probably a good idea. But first he tells me he has to put his shopping away and this takes him nearly ten minutes. And then he drives so slowly I want to scream at him. I hold it back but I don't know how. You don't get a second shot at this. He keeps talking but I'm not listening. If only he would shut up.

A black taxi pulls in at the same time as us and a man jumps out, slamming the door behind him. It's Charlie. We run down the corridor together, my legs as heavy as lead.

Emma is sitting beside you, holding your hand. She looks up anxiously and moves her chair back to make room for me. I gently take your hand in mine, for a moment surprised there is no resistance on your part. You take two more shallow breaths and then stop breathing. Charlie leans over to kiss your forehead and then leaves. I kiss your hand and stroke your face, drinking in every detail of you. It's been three months since I last saw you. 'I love you, darling.' Can you hear me? You are still warm but you are not coming back to us.

Emma says that only yesterday you asked for your bed to be turned around so it faces the window. You wanted to be able to see the trees. Oh, my love.

The nurse tells us there is another room where we can take you. I so need more time with you. Emma gathers up some of your things, including the painting of the dove, your dream catcher and some candles. The three of us then begin wheeling you down the corridor. We pass the nurses in reception. No one looks up when your body passes by. I would have liked them to honour your body in some way. The new room is empty of furniture apart from a few chairs. I speak softly and whisper goodbye to you and am strangely sure that you can hear me.

'Don't be afraid, Jasmine. You are leaving this world and crossing over to the other side.'

I feel calmer for being with you. The hours pass. Emma and I talk a little. There is a slight gap in the curtains and when a faint glimmer of dawn appears, Emma suggests that we might go home soon. You seem peaceful. Are you?

'Yes, okay, we can go shortly; however, I have to phone an undertaker first. I've chosen a small firm... a husband

and wife team who I like the sound of. I hope my choice is a good one.'

Within the hour, two men pushing a trolley appear from the far end of the corridor. They are wearing ties and dark clothes. I need to talk to them first because I want them to call you by your name, as you will be able to hear them. They seem nice. I show them into your room and they bring the trolley. What happens now? I haven't given this any thought. I hear one of them counting quietly, and on a count of three, they lift you off the bed and place you on their trolley. I will never forget the sound of the zip. Emma asks them not to cover your face. We stand side by side, watching you being wheeled out of the room, through a side door and outside into a cold December morning.

Emma and I slowly make our way to the reception area. The corridor seems longer than usual. A nurse is there to meet us. She is the one who tucked you into bed at night, and although not supposed to, she always kissed you goodnight. I like knowing things like that. She gives us each a hug and tells me again how fond she was of you. The sliding doors part and Emma and I step outside. There's no sign of a moon or any light from the stars. Instead, thick clouds hang over us like brooding ghosts.

Charlie went back to tell Josh and Penny that you have died. They knew you were very ill, but I don't think they considered that you would die. Those poor children; they are so young to have the death of a special aunt. They have drawn pictures of you and leave them on the bottom step for us to see. It is Charlie's idea. They have written down all the reasons they love you... they love you because you sing and play your guitar and get them joining in. They love painting and making things with you. Josh writes that you are a special aunt and that you love each other.

Emma comes to tell me that she is going to bed. Her footsteps are slow and sound weary going up the stairs. Poor darling, she is exhausted. The house is so quiet… it doesn't feel right. Why aren't we all crying? And the owls; why aren't they hooting with dismay? They must surely know you have died. I don't go to bed. What's the point? I make tea and watch another sliver of light stealing across the sky.

Dare I go in your room? I stand in the doorway. It still feels like yours. Even after the twenty-eight days while you were in the hospice, a lingering trace of your fragrance remains. Pieces of your make-up are on the mantelpiece, and some of your hair is entwined in an overturned brush. I slide the top off a lipstick, hoping to be able to sense you there.

What happens now? How will life go on without you? I can't imagine that it will.

Love,

Mum

10th Dec, 2013, 5pm

Ja... , my love,

Alan is coming to collect me, as we have an appointment with the funeral director. We will obviously be discussing arrangements for your funeral service, and I want to see your body again. I'm a bit nervous about it. How will you look?

Alan's driving is still a bit erratic. He doesn't slow down before roundabouts; however, unlike all those years ago when I attempted to teach him to drive, I keep a diplomatic silence! I think you would be proud of me. We need petrol so he pulls over into the next garage. He's more agitated than I realised because he inadvertently splashes petrol over his raincoat. Cross, he takes off the coat, then rolls it into a tight ball and puts it on the back seat of the car. You can imagine the stench! 'One cremation is quite enough,' I tell him. I hope this doesn't offend you, Jasmine. I don't quite understand how humour finds its way in like that. We relax a little more. He puts his coat in the boot. Unable to make small talk, we lapsed into silence.

What with the delay at the petrol station and the stinking raincoat, we arrived late and somewhat dishevelled for our appointment. The funeral director very kindly puts us at our ease and we sit around a low table while he makes tea for us. He reaches for a large pad and begins asking a few questions. Do we want you brought to your funeral in a black hearse? Instinctively, it doesn't feel right. I tell him that you love colour, so he's going to bring you in his silver saloon car.

That's much better. And we would like you carried in by four men who know and love you. Alan will ask one of his brothers and I will ask one of mine. Your cousin Adrian and Neil, your best friend, will be the other two.

The arrangements are falling nicely into place but it's the venue that concerns me. The local crematorium leaves me cold and we wouldn't be allowed to decorate it and make it beautiful for you.

'Is there anywhere else we can use?' I ask.

He sits thoughtfully, drumming his fingertips on the pad.

'Well, there is a little chapel in the grounds of another crematorium and if it's free you can have it for as long as you want and decorate it as you please.' He will know the next day if it's available.

And then it's time for me to see you, Jasmine. I'm nervous. The director very kindly held out his hand and I accepted it gratefully.

Love,

Mum

Jasmine, darling,

Hilary and her husband, together with Linda, are the first to arrive at the chapel. Linda brings her cello and Norman has agreed to play the organ for us. I am so relieved to see them. The chapel door is unlocked, and although the heating is on, it feels rather chilly. Norman looks around for the organ. We chuckle when we realise there simply isn't one. Thank goodness we have Linda and her cello.

Cousin Adrian is the next to arrive. Having driven via your flat to fetch some of your paintings, he then helps us to arrange them along the windowsills. Your largest one of the dolphins tumbling in the sea is too big for that, so we stand it on the floor leaning against the altar table. Hilary covers the table with a blue velvet cloth and I arrange some fresh flowers. We light a number of candles and place them on the table and around the window ledges, then stand back to see the effect. The chapel shimmers in soft pools of candlelight, and the flowers and vibrant colours of your paintings lend the final touches. It looks beautiful. People have begun arriving.

Unlike a wedding, you never know who will come to a funeral. I am so pleased to have old friends with us. We hug each other, for a brief moment forgetting that we are here for your funeral. Neighbours who have known you and Emma since you were small slip into the back pew. I recognise two of your school friends looking much the same as they did all those years ago. How kind that two of the hospice nurses have come, one of whom was your night nurse. Cousins I haven't seen for a number of years arrive, bringing their youngest member, who is just six months old.

Your father and I sit on a front pew with Emma between us. The doors of the chapel open and the chatter drops away. The four men walk in slowly, carrying your willow basket on their shoulders. Hilary stands up and steps forward. Linda, seated in the centre of the nave, draws herself up, raises her bow and begins playing. Sublime cello sounds weave their way into our already vulnerable hearts. The pale winter sun pours through an overhead window and wraps Linda in tiny coloured sunbeams. The men place your coffin on the ancient slabs. It is so close to me I could reach over and touch it.

Hilary welcomes us all. Her words are simple yet profound. She talks about love and the love we feel for you. I shall of course keep the transcript of it.

Emma and cousin Adrian are the first to get up to speak about you. They stand side by side, no doubt feeling stronger because they are together. Emma recounts some of her childhood memories. I didn't know you used to copy her choice of ice cream flavour. Regardless of what it was, you always wanted the same. This went on for quite some time. The day inevitably came when you wanted to choose your own flavour. It marked a more independent stage in your growing up, though Emma tells us she missed your allegiance. The two of you had plenty of arguments, but the love between you remained constant.

Adrian is next. Six months ago, he drove you to a recording studio for you to record two of your songs. He brings out a small CD player and presses a button. It is you playing your guitar and your voice is soaring. I haven't heard this song before. I'll listen to it again later, though not yet. It's much too soon.

Hilary invites me to come forward. I call inwardly for strength and get up slowly, listening to the echo of my heels clicking on the slabs. I wonder if anyone can see my hands trembling. I want to tell everyone about your creativity, and how important it was to you, both in your artwork and in the gardens you loved restoring.

There were a number of stories I could have shared but there isn't time for all of them. So I don't mention your elderly neighbour with a very overgrown garden, and how after work you knocked on his door, offering to clear it for him. I would love to have seen the response on his face! It takes you several days and then you go round and sow some seeds and water them regularly. His garden blooms and he is often seen outside, snoozing in a deckchair, surrounded by his flowers.

Nor do I tell them about the man from the Samaritans who knocked at my door. I was on the point of saying 'No, thanks,' when you appeared. You tell him you want to donate because you know what it feels like to wake up scared in the middle of the night when there is no one to talk to.

But I do tell them how much you care about people who are less fortunate. Every week, you bought a copy of the *Big Issue,* even when it left you a little short of money. Jasmine, I can't walk past someone selling the magazine without doing the same. I can almost hear you nudging me!

And I do mention your resoluteness and how at times it served you well, though at other times less so. I am surprised when I hear ripples of laughter gathering. Jasmine, by now

I am so enjoying talking about you, bringing you back to life.

You will remember the poem *Shining Light* that you wrote after my mother died. You sang it at her funeral. Well, I'm going to read it out now. Linda has agreed to improvise the choruses on her cello, just like you did on your guitar.

Shining Light

"I wish you were the wind, so I could touch you
I wish you were the sunshine, so I could feel you
I wish you were the seasons, so I could watch you bloom
I wish you were the birds, so I could hear your song.

I wish you were the water, so I could be moved by you
I wish you were the earth, so I could heal you
I wish you were the sky, so I could admire your light
I wish you were the music, so I could let you in.

When I look at the mountains, they remind me
Of your strength and courage to see it through
Now you're crossing waters, your heart full of trust
Like a golden eagle, you look down upon us.

Shining Light"

Hilary then invites each of us to come forward and select a rose to place on your coffin. This will be our last goodbye to you. I am to lead the way. I choose one that is deep red, the same colour as the roses on the bush you gave me.

You and Emma both grew up appreciating roses. When

you were about eight and Emma eleven, you decide to have a go at making rose perfume. First, you gather all the fallen rose petals from the garden, then you carefully wash them and leave them soaking in clean water. Three days might have been better than two, but you are both a little impatient! After carefully pouring the fragrant water into small plastic bottles, you decide to have a little stall at the front of the house. A number of passers-by stop and chat with you both and some purchase a bottle of rose water. By the end of the afternoon, you have sold the lot and in the process amassed the princely sum of fourteen pounds and fifteen shillings. That was a lot of money in the eighties. You decide to donate the proceeds to the Blind Society, because Mr Brown, our piano tuner, is blind and he really impressed you. When you receive a letter thanking you both for your efforts, you are thrilled.

Jasmine, the funeral director says your funeral was one of the most moving ones he has ever attended. He is such a genuine man that I like to think that he means what he says and is not just being polite.

Afterwards, we gather in the local pub. I can't eat a thing, though I am grateful when someone hands me a large glass of red wine. The pillar in the middle of the room makes it an ideal venue for a funeral reception with divorced parents. The family of my ex-husband gather on one side, while mine converge on the other. Emma sits uncomfortably on a stool at the bar, midway between the two. I feel very proud of my brothers when they step over the unspoken boundary to mingle with the "other side".

A few of us go back to the house. Your cousin joins us and also Sue, your artist friend, who of course brings her little black poodle, Money. I don't want them to go. Can't we just carry on talking like this?

Were you pleased with how your service went? I do hope so.

Love,

Mum

Sweetheart,

I doubt I will ever stop thinking about you. Have you safely left this world and crossed over into the next? I have one last appointment with the chaplain and after that I shall wend my way home. I'm not looking forward to getting back, knowing that you will not be there. I'm just about functioning, though not yet firing on all cylinders. I'm still wrapped in a bubble of shock, frozen and numb inside.

It feels weird going to the hospice without you being there. Muppet stays in the car. The chaplain is at reception waiting for me. On our way to the chapel we pass "your" room and I find myself help wondering who is occupying it now. Just then a tall, rather thin man comes out, closes the door behind him, brushing away a tear.

I tell the chaplain how dreadful I feel. 'Of course you do,' he says, and when I say how uncertain I am of any future without you, he nods. And then we talk about grief.

'Let it rip!' he advises. 'This pain is love. Allow the grief to unfold in whatever way it wants to. There is a healthy pain associated with grieving that will dissolve in time. However, when grief is held back and not expressed, the emotions stay locked in the body and can cause physical and emotional illness. So allow yourself to feel everything.'

With his encouragement, I let go a little more. The knot in my stomach slowly uncurls and I cry and cry. I shall be sad saying goodbye to the chaplain, and although he says I can come back any time, I know I won't. We are done now.

I needed to be reminded that it is healthy to grieve, because in my family we never showed our feelings, let alone talked about them. If anything, feelings were seen as weakness. My parents were the war generation, so stoicism and a "stiff upper lip" were very much the order of the day. As an army officer my father was well trained in this, though it must have been difficult for him at times, as he was a deeply sensitive man, a poet and a writer. Whenever I went to stay, it was always dad who picked flowers from the garden and arranged them in a vase by my bed.

I have a lot to think about on my journey home. There's no rush. I find myself appreciating the beauty of the crisp, white covering on the ground, the frosted branches of trees and the sense of stillness that comes in winter when everything slows down. Muppet sleeps most of the way home and wakes just as we turn into my road.

'How will we manage without Jasmine, Muppet?' He looks up at me and barks. I swear that dog is nearly human. Although his eyes are clouding over with cataracts, he is still lively and his presence is enormously comforting. I am so glad to have him.

Love,

Mum

Dear Jasmine,

Another year is here. I don't remember much about Christmas and I'm relieved it's over. I take with me the kindness of my brother and sister-in-law, my niece and nephews. And now I'm gearing myself up to clear and clean your flat. I'm not looking forward to it. Emma wants to sort through your clothes and Adrian will dismantle your bed so that Emma can take it back for Josh. My brother is on standby in case I need extra help.

I am the first to arrive. Although I have a front door key, I don't want to go in on my own, so I go round the back to look at your garden. Someone must have dug the vegetable patch for you, as you wouldn't have had the strength to do it on your own. Whoever it is, thank you. Even in winter, the garden looks lovely. The potato and cabbage plants are doing well, and it was a good idea putting the pots of herbs along the fence to give them wind protection. Your secateurs with the bright yellow handles are on the shelf in your little greenhouse. 'I won't be able to lose them,' you tell me. I see there's also a pink trowel, a ball of string and several refolded seed packets.

The bird tray was my house-warming gift; however, the pigeons annoy you as they take more than their fair share. I will bring it home and when the weather warms up I want to create a special corner for you in the garden. Your dolphin stone will sit nicely on your little bench – you were so excited when you found it lying in the corner of a field. 'Look, it already has the shape of a dolphin head and the little hole is just like an eye.'

I hear cars pulling up. Emma and Adrian both arrive at the same time. The three of us go in together. My breath catches when I see your dancing shoes in the hall. There are three pairs – a gold pair with thin straps, a silver pair and a pretty, red pair with flowers on the fronts. The heels are a bit scuffed, so I expect you danced in them a lot.

When you were eight, I tried to interest you in ballet classes. As a child, I enjoyed ballet so much that I thought you might too. You gave it a go, but when a new TV series of *Tarzan* clashes with the ballet, *Tarzan* wins hands down.

When I was twelve, my ballet teacher encouraged me to apply for a place at the Royal Ballet School. I was invited for an audition. The other dancers seemed a million miles better than me, so my confidence wobbled. At the end of a long day, a rather serious adjudicator wearing thick-rimmed glasses informed me that I was going to be too tall for ballet. I wondered if she was just being polite. So instead of going to ballet school, my parents sent me to an all girls' boarding school, where every new girl was teased about something or other. Because of ballet my feet turned out when I walked, so not surprisingly, my nick-name was Duck Feet!

When you were thirty-two, you fell in love twice. First, with the tango dance, and shortly after that you met and fell in love with a handsome Portuguese man. Your friendship blossomed and you were very happy together. However, five years later it all came to an end. Although you remained friends, you were very sad about it. After you died, Emma tried to contact him on Facebook, but without any success.

We didn't come across your beautiful dance dresses in your bedroom wardrobe. I wonder where they are; however, we did find the red coat, cream blouse and yellow cardigan that you bought on your last shopping spree with Emma. You wore the coat home and twirled around in front of us, telling us that the colour red will lift you. That was just two months after you were diagnosed with cancer.

Adrian asked if he can take your drum and piano keyboard home for his boys. 'Yes, of course.' However, I regretted this later as the drum skin is alive, so it will have had your essence in it.

I'm strangely pleased when they both leave, as I want to be alone in the flat. Even after these three months since you left, I have the strangest feeling that you might walk in at any moment. You will look puzzled to see me here, and then you will be annoyed to see me clearing away your belongings. It's a terrible thought that I am here to clear you away, to leave no trace of you, when it's the last thing I want to do.

When I see a splodge of blue paint on the carpet, I feel absurdly happy. How ironic that I will now have to try and remove it. And look, there's a little jar of pink nail varnish on the table and you haven't secured the top properly. It's already hardened. No matter, I tighten it. As I turn to go into the kitchen, I notice a door I haven't seen before. It's a cupboard, and on the floor, stacked against each other, are a number of paintings. Each one is framed and ready to hang. I haven't seen any of them before. Goodness, you have been busy preparing for your exhibition. I'm so sorry your plans have been cut short, as it would have made you very happy. You were so excited at the thought of having an open evening.

Which books were you last reading? I trace the spines in the bookcase but am left none the wiser. Just at that moment, I catch sight of the little purse I brought you back from Ecuador. It is tucked at the end beside a book. I'm so glad you kept it all this time. I take it out, marvelling at the intricacy of such tiny coloured beads threaded together by the indigenous women. I remember telling you that I had a go at beading myself. It was much harder than I imagined. And as for collecting and sieving the beads from the bottom of the river, it takes ages.

I never asked you what it was like having a mother who loves to travel and meet indigenous people. It is another of those conversations I wish we'd had.

Although it's getting dark, I don't want to put a lamp on. Neither do I want to leave your flat. If your bed was still here, I would sleep there. Instead, I curl up on your rug in the last of the light. I know that if I was with the tribe, the women would gather around me and take it in turns to watch over me. For them, grieving is an honourable and wholesome response to loss, and the person is supported throughout their process.

If only it was like that here.

Love,

Mum

16th Feb, 2014, 3am

Jasmine,

I'm in agony and spend ages just sitting on the sofa. It's hard to describe how I feel. I've no energy for anything. Muppet needs a walk each day but that's about it. I can't get warm, even with a hot water bottle in my back. Anna has been over. You met her on a few occasions. She hands me a card and a small gift. I make tea for us. I want to talk about you, so tell her a little about your funeral. Then we cry together. I didn't see her again after that. It takes me a little while to put two and two together, and then I remember that her greatest fear is that something awful might befall her own daughter, and here am I showing her that such a dreadful thing can, and sometimes does, happen.

A couple of neighbours bring me cards, and since I'm relatively new to the area, I am surprised and grateful. The lady opposite also calls by and tells me to knock on her door if ever I am in need of company and a cup of tea. I appreciate that.

Love,

Mum

Treasure,

Can you believe it? I went to the gym a few days ago. What an effort, even though it's only across the road. My body is so stiff that I thought that some fast-ish walking on the treadmill might help. The machines look out over the playing fields of a school. This morning, two fair-haired girls aged about nine or ten came running across the field in my direction. They were wearing the same coloured blazer as you used to at that age. One of them even looked like you. I had to stop and go home. I doubt I will go again. It was too much too soon.

Now there's something I want to tell you, as I don't want it festering. After you died and we moved your body into the other room, I sang to you and wished you a safe journey to the other side. My huge regret is that I didn't climb onto the bed beside you and hold you in my arms. I wanted to very badly but something stopped me. I remember thinking there might not be enough room on the bed for me, or that a nurse might come in and tell me it wasn't allowed. How ridiculous is that! Anyway, I'm glad I've shared it with you. I wish I could go back in time.

You didn't want any medication, did you? I guess you wanted to be in charge as much as possible. You had such courage and determination and such anxiety too. My sense of shock is wearing off, which is quite hard, as it means I'm feeling everything more.

It will soon be Mother's Day and I'm trying to prepare myself for the fact that there will only be one card. How do I prepare myself for that? This is the beginning of a whole series of firsts without you.

Love,

Mum

Dear Jasmine,

I ache with missing you. When I hear Emma's card drop onto the mat in the hall, I nearly run after the postman and tell him he must surely have another one in his bag. I manage to restrain myself, thank goodness. In the afternoon, there is a knock at the door and a man from the flower shop hands me a most beautiful bunch of flowers. It is so kind of Emma to think of me when she too is grieving for her sister. I'm thankful the day is over. Normally, you're the one who writes poetry but I wrote you a few lines.

Mothering Sunday

"Howling to the moon, I wonder
Do you sit on a star?
Or sleep in a cloud?
Where are you?
Come back just for five minutes
So I can hear your voice.
Let us take time
To say all the things
We never said
When you were alive."

Love,

Mum

Sweetheart,

I'm blown away by what happened earlier. As you will know, I have a little routine in the mornings. It's very simple… I make a cup of tea, light a couple of candles and place one either side of your photo. Then I sit and allow my thoughts to drift. They are always about you.

Today will remain with me always. The candles began flickering as if a light breeze had entered the room, yet it's chilly so all the windows are closed. The natural light begins to radiate more brightly and I sense a presence with me. It is like being held in a soft embrace. I hardly dare move in case the feeling goes away.

'You're back,' I whisper, tears rolling down my face.

My head and shoulders are tingling and then something very soft like the back of a hand brushes my cheek. My body trembles. I'm sure I hear you say, 'I'm safe and well, Mum. I needed to rest, but I'm getting stronger.'

Then the light returns to normal and your presence leaves. I can't move with the wonder of it all. How many minutes passed I have no idea. And then I go and spoil it all by wondering if it really was you, or maybe it was all in my imagination. Thoughts and doubts begin tumbling around my head like clothes in a washing machine. I tell them to go away and bring myself back to how I felt.

'Thank you, my darling daughter. Please come again.'

Love,

Mum

Darling,

Yesterday, I had a marvellous treatment with Lucia. I'm so glad to have met her as it means that I finally have some support. I trust her completely. I think it would be very hard to drop into this grief without support in place. I go once a week and she has kindly reduced her fees so I can afford it.

But what I really want to say is thank you for your visit yesterday. You came at the perfect time, as I was lying very relaxed on Lucia's massage table. I felt your presence and this time I was in no doubt that it was you. I heard you say, 'You are so soft now, Mum.' And then you snuggled into me just like you used to as a child. You would burrow your head in my lap and then I scooped you up and turned you upside down. 'More, more,' you squealed. You always wanted more.

Lucia senses you in the room with us, and I so appreciate her being a witness to this. I am sure now that this is no figment of my imagination. I just have to keep trusting and allow whatever is happening to unfold.

Today, I'm back in the pits. Up down, up down. That's how it seems to go. The grief is totally unpredictable and it's tiring work for sure. Sometimes, my sense of despair and hopelessness frighten me. I never know what's going to happen from one day to the next. I don't want to die, but then neither do I want to live.

By the way, I've had your painting of the dolphin framed, and it's on the wall to the left of the window, just across from your painting of the eagle. The dolphin reminds me of you, because of the way he is lifting himself out of the water with such determination.

Sometimes, I'm sure I hear you calling me in the hallway, so I hurry downstairs in case it's you. It never is, of course. Muppet doesn't stir, so I should know better by now, especially as your car isn't parked behind mine.

Muppet gets me out of bed in the mornings. He pads in around eight o'clock. I roll over groaning, as I often don't get to sleep until dawn. Muppet just stands there and if I don't stir, he barks and barks.

This morning, the grey March clouds are so low in the skies there is little possibility of brighter weather. That's fine by me as sunshine is not welcome here. What right does the sun have to even rise in the mornings when you are no longer here? Look, the key to your flat still hangs in the hallway, just in case you ever lose yours. I don't need to hold on to it anymore, but I can't let it go. What if you come back looking for it and it isn't there? Am I losing the plot? You are dead, so of course you won't be coming back. I sit on the bottom of the stairs and weep into the emptiness. I'm a mess.

Love,

Mum

Jasmine,

A nurse friend came round unexpectedly as she had a day off. Normally, she tells me when she's coming over, but this time she doesn't. I'm embarrassed by the state of the kitchen. Unfazed, she finds yellow rubber gloves in the drawer, dons an apron, and then I hear the clanking of washing-up. More than that, she washes the floor and all the surfaces, and I feel enormously grateful. She then heats up the soup that is in the fridge and finds some cheese. It's lovely to be looked after like that. When she goes, I decide to wash up more regularly.

The days and weeks are passing slowly. I long for the darkness, but when it comes I dread going to bed as I sleep so poorly. Grief has taken hold of my mind and my memory is shot to pieces. When I go to the shops, I can't remember what I have gone there for. Sorrow steals everywhere and anywhere it can find a space. My ankles and knees are swelling, and my lungs ache with pains that sometimes make my breathing uncomfortable. But the biggest ache of all is in the centre of my chest where my heart lies broken in a million pieces.

Another ache has appeared, and it's the strangest one of all because it's in my womb. I can make no sense of it, unless it is you tugging at me from the other side. Are we still connected in the way we used to be? It makes me think of that course we went on. It was a weekend all about energy, and even though we can't see energy, we are all connected by it.

There were twelve of us on the course. The exercise that stands out above all others is the one we did in pairs. One person in each pair wears a blindfold. My partner is wearing one, so I move slowly into another part of the room. Her task is to find me purely by tracking my energy. Five other pairs are doing the same. I was standing there waiting for my partner to try and find me, though instead of her coming towards me, it is you. You are holding out your arm and as soon as you touch me you take off your blindfold. We are both amazed! By now, the others are watching the extraordinary connection playing out between a mother and child. This connection begins the moment the child is conveived in the womb, and it continues growing throughout the nine months. I'm now wondering if it continues even after death.

We repeated the exercise a second time, this time with a different partner. Once again, you find me in the room. 'I can always find you, Mum,' you tell me, removing your blindfold.

'Can you? Can you still find me, Jasmine? I hope so.'

Something similar happened between me and my mother. It was around the time of my trip to Ecuador. I decided not to tell her the exact date of my departure, as I know she will only worry. A few days later, I received an email from my brother telling me that on the day of my departure, and within an hour of my flight, Mum fell off her tricycle while bicycling down the road. Fortunately, she was unscathed. It was yet another example of the invisible connection of energy playing out between a mother and her child, albeit an adult.

The pains in my womb last a few weeks longer, until one evening in my bath I notice they have gone. Does this mean we are no longer connected? I hope not. I don't know what to make of it.

Love,

Mum

25th April, 2014, 4pm

Sweetheart,

It was Josh's sixteenth birthday on Tuesday. There was a party in the evening and lots of people were there. I tried to be relatively cheerful and I hope I did okay. He is missing you, as are we all. The drive there and back was, as usual, very pretty but I found it exhausting.

I still can't believe that you are no longer with us. It's as painful as it was weeks ago, more so if anything. The emotions are like waves and they take my breath away, though fortunately, they don't last too long. But the feelings lying deeper in the body last much longer. My poor body is going crazy. I have never known anything like this, and I sometimes wonder if I'm going a little mad with it all.

You fought so hard to keep your life going. Were you scared? You didn't say anything to Emma, who sat with you every afternoon. I wanted to sit with you too but you wouldn't let me. I feel cheated of something more intimate. It would have been so much easier for me if we had said goodbye. A friend of about my age died around the same time as you. She wanted to die on her own, though she first said goodbye to her three daughters and several grandchildren. They were at peace with that.

I clung to the hope of you having another near-death experience. I was grasping at straws. I didn't realise how unhelpful hope is. It kept me looking at the future when all we have is the here and now. This minute, we only have this

minute. You might even have said thank you to Emma…
and maybe to me too, for bearing you, for giving you life,
for holding you, loving you as best I could. I know it wasn't
perfect, but there was always a reason for you to push me
away.

Love,

Mum

Good morning, Jasmine,

I wonder how you are… I think of you every day. Will that ever change, I wonder? Certainly, going to the depths of my grief is life-changing. I'm in a dark hole. Emma suggests I take some medicine to numb my feelings, but it's not my way. I've spent years numbing myself out of sadness by keeping busy, talking on the phone, two or three glasses of wine, a film on television, and so forth. Grief is an expression of love and if I numb myself I will be numbing you too. Mind you, I completely understand others who feel a need to do this.

Yesterday was grim. I think swimming exhausted me and I had to go to bed afterwards. People are scared of grief. They don't know what to say to me so they usually say nothing. I find that hard. I'm tired of being asked if I'm okay when it's obvious I'm not. And it's perfectly okay not to be okay. How could it be otherwise?

I'm aware that one grief is touching another, so my grief for you is having a knock-on effect on the others buried away inside me. Sometimes, I think I am feeling lighter, but then I get knocked down again. Grief is a strange beast, yet I sense a certain beauty around the rawness of it.

I want to tell you about the two dreams I had this morning. It's the first time since you died that I've woken up remembering a dream. In the first dream, I am with friends and we are swimming and frolicking in a pool, laughing like kids. I am carefree and that feels so good.

The second one is even better because you and Emma are in it. The three of us are away somewhere and in the morning, I come into your bedroom with a beautifully wrapped Easter egg and some golden coins in shiny paper. I give them to Emma. She is clearly unimpressed and at that point you both start giggling. You aren't in the least bit bothered that I haven't given you an egg – as if that would have happened! The three of us are laughing so hard that we have to lie down on the bed. I touch your hair and tuck it behind your shoulders. We are so loving and happy together. I wake up feeling very different to how I was before I went to sleep. Ah, such lovely dreams.

I wrote this last night.

Grief

"Deep down in the belly of grief
Streaks of pain tear through me.
Oh mercy. Take pity on my despair.
There is no choice,
The cries of mourning move in strong currents
Pulling out old griefs, losses and guilt,
Cleansing vessels, bones, cells and tissues
Washing them all through,
Preparing to receive and open to the new.

How long will it take? I ask.
A small deep voice within says,
'Fear not, dear one.
You will know when it is done.'"

Will the grief really come to an end? I somehow doubt it.

Love,

Mum

Jasi. ine,

I'm awake quite early and feeling brighter. Instead of staying in pyjamas and dressing gown, I get dressed, make a packed lunch and a flask of coffee, and walk to the lake. It's a nice day. Muppet can't get over me being up early. Perhaps my energy is returning... mind you, I've thought this before. Up down, up down.

One or two friends are inviting me over and I can just about cope with one-to-one. Some can't bear it when I bring you into a conversation. I think I need to explain that I want to talk about you. It's like a slap in the face when the subject of you is dropped or avoided. I'm in a different world to everyone else. I'm in between worlds, neither here with them nor there with you.

Large groups and noisy places are impossible so I avoid them. While I don't want to isolate myself, in many ways it's easier to stay on my own; however, it makes this a very lonely business.

Spring has well and truly sprung and the bulbs I planted when you were poorly are shooting up. Did I really plant all this stuff? The daffodils are out and the tulips are about to open. Wild primroses and foxgloves have appeared from nowhere, no doubt carried in by the birds. I wish they hadn't bothered. Spring is an affront. I want to cancel it and make it leave the garden. On the other hand, I love watching the birds. Chaffinches dart in and out of the hedgerows in search of grubs and the like, and the swallows are arriving. In the afternoons, they gather in the poplar at the back. The rooks are the bosses and it only takes one to land in the tree to send them all scattering. Before long, the swallows come back and the chase begins all over again. I look for you in the skies. Oh, for another word from you. It is almost warm enough to sit out. I like sitting beside the pond. I hope a dragonfly will come, though it's probably not quite warm enough yet.

Sundays are the worst days. Dare I visit the neighbour opposite who invited me to call round? As far as I can see, they have no visitors. I would love a cup of tea but mainly a bit of company. I pluck up the courage and go and knock on their door. She is surprised to see me, and then her grandson, aged about seven or eight, appears and grins. 'Hello,' he says cheerily. His front teeth are missing. She tells me she's sorry but this is not a convenient time to call and then closes the door. I feel mortified and slink home, vowing never to do that again.

Love,

Mum

18th May, 2014, 10pm

My love,

Ah, yesterday, you made your presence felt in a completely different way. I was in bed early, exhausted as usual from the emotional swings of the day. I heard a loud thud just outside my bedroom and at first I wondered if Muppet had bumped into something. Alternatively, we might have an intruder. I tentatively push back the bedclothes and open the door. Muppet is still in his basket and hasn't stirred and there is no sign of anyone. However, your canvas painting is lying on the floor. The nail is still firmly in place, yet somehow the picture has dropped off. This is you, isn't it, Jasmine? There is no way it could have dropped off on its own. I smiled and went back to bed.

'Thank you, Jasmine. Good night, sweetheart.'

I slept better than usual that night. It's as if you are watching over me, finding different ways to show me that you are around. When I feel low, I tell myself that you are not far away. My whole world seems to be expanding, because here I am on Earth linking with you in the world of Spirit. It's an extraordinary feeling, knowing that our two worlds can come together like this.

I'm spending the weekend with the family so I'll write again after that. I wonder if you will find a way to link with Emma. She misses you very much.

Love,

Mum

Jasmine,

I wonder how you are… Do you hang out with other members of the family there? I have no idea how it works. I hope you are not lonely. I'm just back from Emma's. It was a long drive. The children miss you. Josh loves talking about you, though Penny is a little more reserved. After they go up to bed, I usually pop my head round the door to say goodnight. Josh has his headphones on – you know how happy he is in his world of music. He waves me in. Goodness knows what prompts me, but I find myself asking him if he has heard from you recently. He grins, nodding. 'Yes, Jasmine was here the other night. I was asleep and she came into my room with her paints and easel. She wanted to say hello to me.' Well, I tell you, I nearly have to sit down! Josh isn't in the least bit surprised by my question.

'What happened next, Josh?' His eyes are twinkling.

'Jasmine begins painting a picture right here beside my bed!' I look astonished and he laughs.

'And what did she paint?'

'It was a picture of a white house and there were lots of flowers in the fields.'

'I wonder if that's where Jasmine is living now,' I muse. 'It sounds nice, doesn't it, Josh? Maybe she is settling.'

Josh nods and returns to his headphones, his head moving in rhythm with the music. With that, I wave him goodnight.

It was lovely to see them but I'm glad to be home. I have another session with Lucia tomorrow. Her treatments are helping me so much. My body feels more relaxed afterwards. You seem to enjoy visiting when I am with her. Maybe it's because I am lying still and relaxed. During the last session, we both felt your presence in the room. This time, you were more animated.

'The music here is exquisite. And as for the colours, they are much brighter than anything you have on Earth... except for maybe one exception... the stained glass windows of Chartres Cathedral.' Are you teasing me? I know I used to go on and on about the beauty of the colours of the windows!

You are not done yet. Only a day or two later, I go into the bathroom and the smallest of your canvas paintings literally drops off the wall. I catch it in my hands! This is your picture of two baby dolphins circling each other in the sea. You used to talk about the different ways they communicate with each other. Is this what you are doing with me?

You have recently begun to make the lamp in the sitting room flicker, though there's no pattern as to when you do this. I've checked the connection and it's not faulty, so I'm sure it's you. Although I feel uplifted when you do this, it also makes me sad, as I long to see you. Your signs are coming quite regularly, so I am wondering if there is something more you want to tell me. Frannie, a friend in France, suggests I might consider seeing a medium at some point. Her husband died suddenly, only two years after they were married. She was desperate for contact with him and did a lot of research to find the right medium to work with her. A medium is someone who is able to communicate with a deceased person in Spirit and if they have a message, she conveys it back to the recipient. I've never thought about this before so I shall ponder it.

Love,

Mum

Sweetheart,

I can hardly believe how I felt when I woke this morning. I was eager to be up and dressed. This is the second time since you died that I've felt so alive and full of a sense of purpose. My intention is to drive over to your flat. It may not sound like much, but it was to me. Where do such ideas come from? Where will I park? It has always been tricky navigating the narrow lanes, never mind finding a space to park. Then I swear I hear you telling me to park further away in a more convenient place. It's a good idea so I do just that. I am preparing myself for the fact that your red car will not be there. Parking was never your strong point so your car was never parked parallel to the kerb like the others. How I long to see it jutting out like it always used to.

Were you happy that we gave your car to your buddy Neil? We thought it was what you would have wanted. It was perfect timing as his had just broken down. I found a passport photograph of you in the front pocket so left it for him on the front seat. Neil was so pleased. Although an inveterate smoker, he tells me he won't smoke in your car because he doesn't want to lose the scent of you.

I stand on the road looking down at your flat, feeling as if I'm in a dream. I half-expect you to come out of the front door and wave. I would like to go and knock on your door and tell the new occupants that you lived there not so long ago. I expect they would look surprised, or even disinterested, but on the other hand, they might invite me in for a cup of tea and then I could tell them all about you. But my feet won't move, so I stand there motionless, rooted to the ground.

I hear a honking sound and look up to see a flight of wild geese, their necks long and outstretched, heading towards the sun. Unlike me, they know exactly where they are going, whereas I am just drifting through the days, longing for nightfall when I can disappear under the bedclothes. A future without you remains unimaginable.

It doesn't seem that long ago since we moved you into the flat. We all helped and it was a great day. Emma sources some pieces of furniture, then hires a van and Neil helps her to bring it over. Emma obviously tells Neil the news about your health. I see him faltering at the door, clearly nervous about what to expect, then he takes a deep breath, goes in and gives you a bear hug. Even though he manages to hide his sadness quite well, he smokes far more cigarettes than usual. I remember you sitting on your new sofa, looking radiant.

'The standard lamp can go in the corner behind the sofa,' Emma says. Then Neil brings in a folding table and a colourful rug. I have a couple of chairs, some crockery and a corner cabinet. A friend of Emma's donates a bed.

Later that morning, a friend of yours comes over to lend a hand, so by now we are quite a party. I have prepared a pasta dish with a vegetable topping, served with lashings of grated cheese and Greek yoghurt. You look so happy with your new home taking shape around you. You have everything you need. Everything, that is, apart from your health.

What was I hoping for by revisiting your flat? I really

don't know. But I do know that a number of memories which I thought were lost to me have returned. So while coming here seems a tiny step, it is in fact huge. A few strands of your short, precious life have come back, and I go home feeling stronger and less fractured.

That night, I dream of long-necked geese flying purposefully towards the sun, and although in the morning I find myself back in the well of sorrow, something indefinable has shifted. I hold fast to the thought that maybe I will eventually find a way of being in this life without you, because unless this happens I don't see much point in anything.

Love,

Mum

Dear Jasmine,

Guilt has been rearing its head. I've tried pushing it away but it won't have it. If anything, it just makes it worse. It's dragging me down and making me feel small. I've felt guilty in the past; I mean, who hasn't? But this time it's acute and it's getting me down. The bottom line is that I feel a failure as a mother, and it's also making me feel worthless as a person. Could I have done more for you when you were growing up, and why wasn't I there to protect you when you were molested? Not enough. Not enough. Just not good enough.

The nights are the worst. Last night, I had a vivid and unpleasant dream where I am standing in court and the judge is about to pass sentence. Looking very severe, he places a white curly wig on his nearly bald head, raises a large hammer and brings it down with great force on the table… 'You are a failed mother,' he pronounces solemnly. 'And the verdict is guilty.' I wake up before he can tell me what my sentence is. God, this is awful. Yes, I know I could have done some things better. I'm so sorry, Jasmine, but does being a failed mother mean that I'm a worthless person? Surely the two are different? Yes, one is my sense of guilt and the other, feeling worthless, is my sense of shame. Yuck.

I phone Hilary. The guilt needs addressing because if anything it's worsening. I don't want it festering in the recesses of my mind, as it'll only leap out when I am least expecting it, or when I'm tired. Hilary invites me over. I'm sure she will have some ideas.

Although it's a bright day, the wind is a little chilly, so we go out into the garden with a blanket each. Their garden overlooks the canal and just seeing the water is soothing. Three or four barges chug past, and people on board smile and wave at us. They are far too cheerful for my liking.

'Write to Jasmine and tell her how you are feeling,' Hilary says.

'But I write to her all the time.'

'Yes, but do you tell her about your wretched sense of guilt and your belief that you are a failed mother?' I shake my head. Hilary is not letting me off this writing task. 'Write down all your thoughts about guilt and shame and continue until they are all down on the page. Here is paper and a pen.'

Goodness, she is well prepared. I don't know how long I wrote for but I filled several large pages. I had no idea there was such a backlog of guilt. No wonder it's been spilling over and what a relief to be addressing it now.

Two significant things happened when I was at boarding school, which I'd like to tell you about, Jasmine, so this may be rather a long letter. Every Sunday, we traipsed in crocodile formation down to the cathedral, wearing the usual drab navy blue uniform with a straight skirt well below our knees. We sit on one side of the aisle while the boys from the grammar school sit on the other. Surreptitious glances and smiles and the occasional letter pass between us.

One Sunday, I find myself quite unable to join in reciting the prayers, as they no longer held any meaning for me. I tell myself that I am not a sinner in need of redemption, that I'm doing my best and I don't need to be forgiven for this. So Jasmine, from that Sunday onwards, I stop saying prayers. Instead, I mouth them silently. However, I'm scared I will be punished or even struck down by the Almighty. Mind you, surely if he is a God of love, as I believe him to be, then this won't happen. Weeks pass and I'm not struck down; however, I'm left with a terrible sense of guilt for turning away from God.

The second thing that took place was soon after this. It was in the aftermath of *Lady Chatterley's Lover*, the novel by D.H. Lawrence, banned in Great Britain in the early sixties. Somebody found a copy on their parents' bookshelves and smuggled it into school. We used to take turns reading it under the bedclothes by torchlight. After a few nights of this, I decide I will have a go at writing my own story. Having promised my school friends something a bit racy I notice my popularity going up a notch.

I usually manage to finish a chapter by Friday; however, distributing it between the desks is quite another matter, as Miss Robarts, supervising the sacrosanct hour of homework, doesn't miss a trick. Three chapters have safely made the rounds. My classmates are longing for chapter four because boy has met girl in an art gallery in Paris and their attraction is electric. It is done. I'm on the verge of passing the chapter under the desk to the girl in front, when Miss Robarts stands up, staring directly at me. Who or what has alerted her? My face turns crimson.

'Bring me everything on your desk,' she snaps. I get up, shaking. Miss Robarts snatches the chapters from me and marches out, clutching them to her enormous bosom.

Chapter four offends both Miss Robarts and the Head. I am summoned to the Head's office. Barely able to look at me, the Head slowly reads aloud the sentence she finds the most offensive: *'The man's hand reaches under her blouse and her nipple hardens.'* I want to shrink and become invisible. Instead, I shuffle from one foot to another, wondering if I'm to be expelled. If that's the case, so be it.

'You should be ashamed of yourself,' she says in a lowered voice. Yes, and more. I feel embarrassed, guilty and ashamed. She then tells me the chapters have been sent to my parents. Oh no, expulsion would have been infinitely preferable! My father is a good writer and the owner of a thriving local bookshop and we both love books. Writing is something we have in common and I want it to stay that way. Perhaps he might even find a fragment of merit in my teenage literary attempts. It's my only hope. Two days later, I go home for the school holidays.

I hear my father climbing the stairs. I've been dreading this. He knocks on the door, then sits at the end of my bed, hardly looking at me. I know then that I am not going to be reprieved. He tells me I shouldn't have written in that way, and then something else that I can't remember because I have frozen. He uncrosses his legs and walks slowly over to the door, and my love for writing slithers away and leaves with him. It will be years before it comes back again.

Hilary asks me to read all this aloud. For a moment I flinch, even from her. Whatever will she think of me? I read it slowly, feeling such compassion for myself, and am struck by the loneliness of my inner world.

Handing me a large box of matches, she asks me to set fire to the pages. The full spectrum of my guilt and shame curls and blackens as the ashes drop onto a plate. 'You don't need this anymore,' she says, instructing me to toss the ashes into the canal. I watch them bob for ages along the water before eventually sinking.

The ceremony was simple, but what depth there is when you are witnessed by a trusted friend. It wouldn't have had the same impact had I done it on my own.

Over lunch Hilary and I reminisce about the day the three of us spent together in the summer. You were full of ideas. First, you want us to drive to the common where a van sells the best ice cream in town. We sit in a row on a large log in the sunshine eating delicious chocolate flavours. Yours begins melting first and you giggle and try to catch it from spilling over.

Our next stop is the nearby pub where we order a pot of tea. We are in no hurry. A bride and groom arrive with all their guests and there is much laughter as they disappear into the dining room.

In the late afternoon, we drive back to town as you want to top up your phone. Since we are not far from an excellent pizza takeaway, you suggest that we order one and take it back to your flat. You seem to know all the best spots to go to. There is a bottle of bubbly in your fridge. I pour us each a glass and it bubbles up our noses making us giggle. Tomato sauce drips onto your jeans and you wipe it away with the back of your hand. We laugh at the mess we are making. We were so happy that day.

Love,

Mum

Dear Jasmine,

The ceremony we did in Hilary's garden was by no means a quick fix; however, my guilt and shame are now exposed and out in the open. I feel different, sort of lighter, and I no longer dread the guilt. Some of the old thoughts still linger, but I'm on the case and I'm approaching it differently. I'm now befriending the guilt and we have little chats together. Guilt's grip is loosening and I feel less weighed down.

I had no idea how much guilt and shame were playing out in my life and I hadn't realised that shame often partners guilt. Guilt is bad enough, but shame is far worse, as it leaves you feeling worthless as a person, that you don't deserve anything, all sorts of toxic stuff like that.

I remember that time when you told me that you felt dirty. I saw the shame in you. Did you see this in me too? Neither of us was able to help the other. Oh, my darling. I wish you were here now. I want to give you a hug. We have so much to talk about.

After my love of writing was shamed out of me due to its sexual overtones, I only wrote when I had to. I continued writing English literature essays at school, though the joy of this had gone. Sex and shame were now intertwined.

In my early forties, a chink of light crept back when I was offered a job writing a monthly feature for a health & fitness magazine. Each month, I focussed on some area of the body, creating exercises the reader could do from home.

I remember suggesting tins of tomatoes as arm weights! It was great fun. Just as the tango found you, writing found me.

Writing to you has made me realise that it wasn't God I turned my back on all those years ago; it was the institution of the Church and the belief that we are sinners. God is all about unconditional love. It's as simple as that. Yet the word *God* turns a lot of people off – it did me at one point, so I tend to use the word *Creator* or *Spirit*. However, right now I don't feel I am loved by God or a Divine Creator. I know that their love is part of who I am; it's just that the thing that's gone walkabout is my love for myself. And until I love and accept myself, I don't think I can let the Creator in. I'm just not there yet.

Love,

Mum

Bloody hell!

I wasn't expecting such anger. It was never welcome in my family; in fact, I never heard my parents argue about anything. Instead, there were long periods of silence during which I wondered what lay at the heart of it. On the few occasions I stamped my feet in exasperation, my mother would tell me not to do that again. 'Being angry just isn't ladylike,' she told me. 'Be nice and keep the peace, and whatever you do, don't rock the boat.'

What happens to all those feelings that have to be pushed back into the body? I couldn't find the words to express my sense of injustice. My rebellious free-spirited nature had nowhere to go, so I pushed it all down again and again. Ironically, I ended up doing more or less what my mother told me to. I was nice even when I didn't want to be. I was good at saying the right things and keeping the peace. On the whole, I kept my opinions to myself, and in time lost touch with what they were. Little by little, the needs of others became more important than my own. And in the process I sold my soul down the river.

So when I wake up full of anger, I don't know what to do with it. There is a rage building inside me that is a monumental backlog of everything I have pushed away. I'm unable to keep the lid on it.

I flounce around the house, inadvertently drop a cup and yell at poor Muppet when he gets under my feet. Muppet doesn't deserve this. I have to take the rage out of the house. My destination will be the lake.

Even when the rain comes down and blurs my view, I head off. The anger is a call back to life. I know I need to follow where it's taking me. Rarely do I meet a soul on the way, which is perfect, as I don't want to have to make any effort, not even to say 'hello' to someone.

If anyone could see me jumping up and down beside the water, they might call me a madwoman. I know I'm not mad. I'm only discharging a lifetime of what has been building up. It needs somewhere to go and I've no desire to dump it on others. I see this happening all too often when someone vents their anger or stirs up an argument with another person.

On one occasion, my yelling frightens off a nearby fisherman. I didn't know he was there until I saw him pack away his fishing tackle and scurry away. As for the poor fish, I imagine they all swam away too. One thing I promise is that I am not going to feel guilty about being angry! It's only noise.

I wasn't expecting to be yelling at you. Off I go to the lake again.

'Why did you have to die? And why did you shut me out when you were dying? It was cruel, so cruel. Were you punishing me? I didn't deserve that.'

On another occasion, my rage was directed at the overworked doctors and nurses in the health service. Even though they were doing their best, they didn't make you better. And when I was done shouting, I dropped to my knees and howled. The birds weren't in the least bit bothered, and the herons didn't stir in the treetops. And as for the ducks and the moorhens, they were far too busy making noises of their own.

Two weeks later, I went back to the lake again. Something else was brewing. This time it was God.

'And as for you, God, where were you when I needed you most? You abandoned me. You're supposed to be a God of love. I stuck up for you because that's what I believe, but let's face it; you don't give a shit about me or my daughter. You are useless!'

I had no idea I felt so abandoned by God. That was when I touched the bottom of my well. Something that was tangled so deeply inside me began to unravel and I dropped to my knees. I am being emptied out. That's the only way I can describe it. This rage is sacred. The toxic self-beliefs of worthlessness and abandonment that have hidden away for so long are at last being pulled out by their roots.

The rage seems to have finished with me, though a low-lying anger rumbles on for some weeks. I'm not always patient with shopkeepers and can feel my irritation mounting when I am kept waiting in what is usually a very reasonable queue of shoppers. I am short-tempered with my brothers when they are kind enough to phone, and I apologise to friends for being grumpy and ask them not to take it personally.

I wish I had known about the lake when you were staying, as you would love it there. Perhaps we might have sat in one of the dips at the water's edge. You would probably bring along your sketchpad. I would make a picnic with a flask of tea and we could while away a few hours watching a heron or two swooping down on a fish, listening to moorhens and ducks chattering around the edges in search of the remains of fishermen's sandwiches. Anger would have been be a million miles away.

Love,

Mum

6th August, 2014, midnight

Dear Jasmine,

I was dreading my first birthday without you, and knew that if I didn't mark it differently it would be unbearable. The days leading up to it are grim. My body begins aching all over, so much so that I worry I am going back to how I was at the outset. Then I remember that the body has its own cellular memory. It forgets nothing. My body knows full well that my birthday is approaching. On the day itself, I was relieved to wake up feeling better. I leave the house before the postman comes, knowing there will be no card from you, and then drive to Bath. Linda and I have lunch sitting outside on the pavement. It is such a different world to where I live, and I am grateful for the contrast. We watch people going by, then huge black clouds begin gathering overhead. A massive storm is approaching. Minutes later, sheets of rain begin deluging down and we run shrieking like children into the nearby Pump Rooms. What a splendid building it is. It is years since I was last here. Relieved to be inside, we have tea like regular tourists, enjoying three musicians playing the cello, the piano and the violin. In the interval, Linda goes over to chat with them. Minutes later, and with huge grins on their faces, they strike up the tune of *Happy Birthday*. Much to my surprise, the day has been wonderful. Thank you, Linda.

It will soon be Emma's birthday and then it will be yours in October. This will be your fortieth. No, you are dead, so it would have been your fortieth. WOULD HAVE BEEN. WOULD, WOULD, WOULD.

You have just made the lamp flicker. Each time you do this, my heart leaps. It is so lovely to hear from you.

Love,

Mum

18th September, 2014, 6pm

Jasmine,

I am just back from dropping Josh at the halfway meeting point in Oxford. Charlie came to meet us. It was so lovely having Josh for the weekend. As you know, he loves playing cards and one of his favourites is the game of "pairs". There we are sitting at the table, he is beating me hands down, when out of the corner of my eye I see the brass lamp that hangs from the ceiling beginning to sway. We stop playing and Josh follows my gaze.

'That's Auntie Jasmine, isn't it?' he says, without a trace of surprise in his voice.

'Yes, I think it is, Josh.'

My heart was racing, I can tell you. Thank you for showing Josh that you are with us. I think it means a lot to him, though it's sometimes hard to tell as his autism prevents a deeper expression. Did you see the smile on his face?

Love,

Mum

10th Oct, 2014, 5am

Sweetheart,

Scattering your ashes as well as marking your fortieth birthday was a lot to do on the same day, though it made practical sense. We wanted it to be special, both for us and for you.

When I arrive, Emma makes me a cup of tea and suggests that we go to the cemetery to see the grave that has been prepared for you. It's a freshly-dug hole with a stick beside it, and your name is written on it with a black felt pen: *Jasmine*. It feels quite shocking, as it is so impersonal, and the hole could have been tidied a bit more. You will be pleased with the position though, because you are near a silver birch and there aren't many trees in the cemetery.

Alan comes over after lunch and he and I lead the short walk to the cemetery. Normally, the person who goes through the kissing gate first turns round to kiss the person behind. However, we do none of that as we are all nervous. Emma carries your ashes and Josh and Penny bring the letters they wrote to you this morning. We gather around your grave and Emma asks me to speak first. I say a few words and ask that the earth be blessed in preparation for receiving you. Then I place the red rose I picked from your bush this morning into the grave. We all take a turn to say something. Josh then reads his letter aloud. It is so full of love for you that we are barely able to speak afterwards. Penny then reads hers.

Emma passes round the container with your ashes and

we scoop out a handful each and scatter them in your grave. There are still plenty left over, so I take out some more and rub them into my hands, feeling the coarseness of them. They remind me of the grainy sand in the cove where we loved to go and swim. It is my favourite beach and the last time we were there I asked you if you would sprinkle my ashes in the sea. See how you have turned around the order of things by dying first.

Still some ashes remain... so I take more out and toss them in the air, loving the feel of them landing in my hair. I don't wash my hair for days afterwards. Then we stand in a circle, your father and I next to each other, and when we hold hands I realise I have forgotten how large his hands are.

Our moods are considerably lighter on the way back. Emma has put so much thought into your birthday ceremony and the scattering of your ashes. We have had a cake made for you. She has piped the number 40 in the middle with your name underneath. It is a work of art. Penny brings down her memory box and shows me all the cards you made her over the years, along with a number of homemade gifts. I am so proud of my grandchildren. Neither has shied away from speaking about you.

A helium balloon has been bobbing against the kitchen ceiling since I arrived. At nine o'clock in the evening, the hour in which you died, we release it outside and watch it drifting up into the night skies beneath a canopy of stars. It has been a big day, and we are stronger for having been together.

What's it like being forty, Jasmine? Did you want a child? I'm unsure, as you never spoke about such things. You did confide in Emma once that you would love a partner and a nice home just like hers. It must be painful reaching an age when having a child becomes more difficult. I know several women at this stage in their lives.

I've woken early today, aware that I have no energy, so I shall just stay in bed under the duvet. It's just one of those days, I guess. Did you like how we marked your birthday?

Love,
Mum

6th Nov, 2014, 8am

My daughter,

It is eleven months since you died. The days seem shorter and darker because you are dying. Even the earth was still as we held our breaths, each day waiting, knowing you will soon die. I don't know what I'm feeling. Nothing. Heavy, just waiting. I'm trying to remember you being happy. Laughing. And I have no memory of you smiling. You are dying slowly, day by day. There is such little time left. Don't die. Please don't die.

Your rose bush has two roses on it. They smell beautiful. I will bring them indoors. I send you my love, as always. Give me the strength to bear this.

Love,

Mum

Darling Jasmine,

Yesterday, we had a beautiful ceremony for the first anniversary of your death. This morning, I was sitting here drinking in the memories of our time together, when a white dove lands on the balcony. He looks directly at me, not down or up, but straight through the window towards me. Rarely does a bird land there and certainly never a dove. It is just like the one you painted flying through a ring of fire into the vastness of the skies. And then he flies off! I wish I'd taken a photo of him but I didn't dare move. He is surely a messenger from the other side. The dove has made my day, my week and probably more.

I'm so pleased I wasn't on my own yesterday. Hilary and Linda spent the day with me, and who better.

I clean the house and prepare the living room with fresh flowers and candles. Hilary brings her harmonium, some red roses and a fine bottle of French wine, and Linda arrives with her cello. Hilary gives a short but moving speech in which she honours me as a mother. She also honours you as my daughter. Then they get out their instruments and begin playing. Nothing has been rehearsed. I love the impromptu nature of this. The three of us begin singing our hearts out. Did you hear our voices soaring? Perhaps you were with us. Afterwards, they peel the petals off the beautiful roses, then joining hands to form an archway, invite me to walk underneath, as they shower me in rose petals, again honouring me as a mother. By now I am crying, though I'm also aware of a huge sense of joy beginning to bubble up. With a great sense of celebration we pour out the wine and toast you, my darling. It is so lovely hearing your name. I have prepared trout stuffed with mushrooms accompanied by new potatoes and a salad. I must say it was delicious. And how we laughed! It never ceases to amaze me how closely allied the tears of sorrow are with tears of joy.

I am learning a lot about the need for ceremony on these anniversaries. In many ways, the simpler they are, the more effective they become. It has been a perfect day in which to remember you.

I hope you enjoyed it too.

Love,

Mum

Sweetheart,

This morning, I bumped into a friend. When she asks me whether I have had closure now that the year is up, I burst into tears. She looks at me aghast, not realising that grief is something that cannot be controlled, and that it continues to twist and turn for as long as it takes. Since grief has no sense of time it doesn't stop when the year is up.

A number of cultures do have a mourning period of one year, during which time female members in the family often wear black. It's possible therefore that the term "closure" has an association with those traditions.

This was certainly the case in Romania where I spent a year doing voluntary work. I was looking for an apartment to rent, and a colleague at work proposed her aunt's flat which would be available in about a week. We arranged to meet there the following day.

The aunt's slippers and various pairs of shoes were lying in the hall, and her kitting was on the table, together with some paper and a pen. The piano was open with a sheet of music on the stand. I assumed the aunt had just popped out for a walk. When I said I was looking forward to meeting her aunt, she threw her head back and laughed. Apparently, her aunt had died nearly a year ago and it is customary to leave the personal belongings of the deceased untouched for a year. The year was up in a week's time so I would be able to move in shortly.

Although a number of her personal effects were cleared away, I was glad to see her paintings still on the wall, and a wonderful collection of old books in the bookcase. I think you and the aunt would have got on famously as you were both artists who loved music. In a way, though, you did get to know her when you and Emma came to stay, because you slept on mattresses in her sitting room absorbing her creativity.

When another friend asks me if I have managed to move on yet, I again burst into tears, though I wasn't quite sure why at the time. Perhaps 'are you still moving through the grief?' would be more appropriate. Words are powerful.

You were very fond of your cousin Polly. She came to stay recently and asked me what she might say to a good friend whose mother died recently. After reflection, she decided on something like... 'I'm so sorry your mum has died. That must be awful for you. I don't know what to say and I don't want to say the wrong thing. I just want you to know that I really do care.'

It is all too easy to walk on the other side of the street in a bid to avoid the discomfort of not knowing what to say to a person who you know is struggling. Yes, we may not get it right; indeed I'm not sure there is a right, but just being present, with a few words or a smile, eases that person's sense of invisibility. And feeling invisible has to be one of the worst feelings in the world.

Goodness, Jasmine. That was a lot of philosophising! Oh I must tell you I walked into town yesterday and caught the bus back as that steep hill is a bit daunting. The neighbour who lives opposite was sitting on the bus. She asks me how I am and I tell her there has been some easing of the anguish.

And then to my surprise she tells me that her own daughter died at the age of four. Well, I am so sorry, I tell her. Perhaps that is why she wasn't able to let me in when I knocked on their door, because my sorrow would have triggered hers, and she is still carrying so much inside her. You never know what people have been through or what sadness they carry in their hearts.

Good night, treasure. Thinking of you as ever.

Love,

Mum

*

Part Three

Afterwards

Dearest Jasmine,

It makes me both happy and sad when you make the lamp flicker … happy because I know you are close by, sad because I still ache with missing you. You've been making the lamp flicker quite a lot recently so I'm wondering if there is more you want to say. Am I on the right track? Anyway, I just sense that now would be a good time to seek the help of a medium. The friend, who worked with a medium after her husband died, highly recommends Sylvia, and that's good enough for me.

I notice that Sylvia is holding a workshop next weekend that is suitable for budding mediums, practising mediums and the curious like me who simply want to know more. There is one place left so I phone and put my name down. 'Well done.' That's what you would say, isn't it Jasmine? A friend has agreed to have Muppet and I manage to book the last room in a nearby hotel. I'm all set to go.

Even though Sylvia put us at our ease, it was a bit daunting being in a group with budding and experienced mediums. I'm the only novice. She tells us that while we all have psychic abilities, we don't necessarily all have mediumship skills. Examples of psychic abilities are when we sometimes sense before picking up the receiver who is calling on the phone, or when we can predict who has just sent a phone text. In other words, sensing something before, or as it happens, is a sign of psychic ability. In 1912, the

Titanic sank and the huge ship went down with hundreds of souls on board. Both before and after the tragedy, people were reporting psychic dreams that had foretold the event. Although it wasn't possible to stop the disaster, some people just knew it would happen. I'm learning such a lot with Sylvia.

Sylvia then has us doing exercises to awaken our psychic awareness and she wants us all to practise mediumship. Holy Moses, I wasn't expecting that!

'How else will you learn? I will be right here if you need any help,' she says on more than one occasion. Sunday is our last day and I am still too nervous to stand up in front of the group. Fortunately, she doesn't let up.

'You've all paid good money to be here, and there are still two people who have not come forward,' she says kindly yet firmly. And of course I am one of them. There is no way out of this, so before my rational mind can come up with a reason not to, I stand up. The group applauds, which makes me feel even more nervous. Sylvia has taught us to wait for someone in Spirit to appear, and although I do just that, no one seems to be coming forward.

'I can't do it,' I tell her.

'Be patient,' she says quietly.

And with that, I see a young woman with long fair hair coming towards me. She has the same build as you, Jasmine. Moreover, she looks about your age. She places a hand inside her blouse and reveals an incision just above her breast. It is just over a year since you died of breast cancer, and now here is this young woman showing me that she died of the same thing. I am amazed at what is unfolding. I tell Sylvia what I am seeing and then walk over to an older woman who is sitting in the front row of the audience. She is crying, as I have just described her daughter. By now I'm crying too. Sylvia then intervenes and tells me it's better to stop now, and that I will feel stronger in the New Year. I return to my seat, humbled that this young woman chose me to communicate with her mother. I'm sure she must know I have experienced the same loss.

Jasmine, can you believe it? Apparently, I have mediumistic abilities. And I bet you were right beside me learning and enjoying every moment. On the strength of the weekend, and the fact that Sylvia is so easy to talk to, I arrange a private Skype reading with her. She's down-to-earth and I like the fact that she smokes cigarettes occasionally and enjoys a glass of wine or two. In other words she doesn't set herself apart as some kind of guru. Normally, she is very booked up; however, someone has just cancelled, so lucky me, as I shall only have to wait a week. Even so, a week is a long time when you are chomping at the bit. You'll be there, won't you? I wonder if anyone else from the family will turn up. I can hardly wait. Perhaps I'll watch a film now as I won't be able to sleep. Which film shall I watch?

'Make it something happy, Mum.' Yes, you are right. I will.

Love,

Mum

19th Dec, 2015, 11pm

Jasmine!

It seems I was right. The frequency of the flickering lamp was you wanting to talk to me. I'm so grateful to Sylvia for her reading, and to you for nudging me to arrange it. Please don't stop being in touch as I couldn't bear it. I'm in a whirl, I can tell you. I've written down everything she said, because even though our session is recorded on my phone, I know I will enjoy reading the words as much as listening to them.

It was the first time I had used Skype so I was quite nervous about it. I was restless all day long, so I'm pleased when Sylvia is prompt. It's nice to see her again. She begins by telling me that while there may be a specific person I want to connect with, we will have to wait and see who comes forward. 'I'm not in charge of any of it. Spirit is.' My fingers are crossed that you will come.

My father is the first to appear. Sylvia describes him accurately – tall and upright – and she seems to know about his military training. Dad is apparently wearing his grey flannel trousers and the tweed jacket with leather elbow patches; the result of my mother's handiwork. Sylvia goes on to describe his personality – quietly spoken with a dry sense of humour, and he enjoyed writing. Again she is very accurate. My father loved nothing better than disappearing into his study to write. Pip, his little dog, followed him in and curled up on his lap. The room filled with pipe tobacco smoke and we could hear the steady tap, tap, tap of the typewriter resonating around the house.

My father has something for me. He is holding out a cushion and on the cushion is a gold pen. The pen is a gift for me as it's time for me to get writing. My father is encouraging me to write! Tears prick my eyes.

My mother also wants to communicate with me. Looking younger than when she died, she is dressed in a pleated skirt and has on her favourite blue sweater. She wants to thank me for all I did for her. 'Thanks, Mum. That's really nice to hear and it means a lot.'

Sylvia chuckles and then tells me there are a few people lining up to see me. My mother's father is next. My Irish grandfather was such fun to be around. He always had a twinkle in his eye, and holding hands we used to skip down the road singing his made-up limericks. The one I liked best was about my long legs turning cartwheels on the grass. He tells me that you are a treasure, Jasmine, and he loves your spontaneity. This is the first word of you. My body tingles and I sit up straighter, praying there will be more.

And then, joy of joys, you are next. Sylvia describes you perfectly – your light brown hair waving slightly, the colour of your eyes and your slim build. I can hardly believe it when she tells me that you had breast cancer, which later spread to your lung. She even describes the treatment you had in hospital.

Sylvia further astonishes me when she describes the clothes Emma and I dressed you in after you died. And apparently, you were at your funeral, and you want me to know how touched you were by our tributes to you, and how much you loved the way we decorated the chapel with your paintings, fresh flowers and candles.

You tell me you are doing your very best to get on with my mother, though it isn't always easy, perhaps because her Irish upbringing was a bit sheltered. Sylvia informs me that sometimes things aren't too dissimilar on the other side as to how they were on Earth! This makes me chuckle.

Sylvia went on to liken your personality to a prickly hedgehog, though she says this is now a thing of the past. You want me to know that, 'Everything gets straightened out over here.' I'm so pleased to hear that and I can imagine you using those words. You also want me to know that you take full responsibility for pushing me away, that you know we could have enjoyed a much closer relationship, and if you were given the chance again, you would do it all very differently. Oh, I can't tell you how much that means, Jasmine. Thank you so much.

Finally, you want to thank me for everything I have done in memory of you, and for all I am still doing, and that you wait for me to say 'Goodnight' to you. Indeed, you have been longing for an opportunity to connect with me, and now you will be able to settle down. I nod. Yes, I think it will be the same for me, darling. Something important has been completed between us.

Love,

Mum

Sweetheart,

I still have some aches around my ribcage, so one of my intentions is to get back to yoga classes. Breathing deeply really helps to move emotions and feelings through the body.

Christmas wasn't easy. How could it be? It's the second Christmas since you died. Nobody mentions your name or speaks about you. I find it unbearable as you are so alive to me. Perhaps I should say something. Will this ever get easier? After lunch, I went upstairs for a couple of hours and had a good howl. I felt better afterwards and came down and joined in playing board games. It certainly focusses the talking and the thinking. I wonder why we don't play them more often. As children, we used to play charades, and that's fun too, as long as you are up to date with books and films and stuff.

I've been feeling up and down ever since, though more down than up.

It wasn't that long ago that you came to France for Christmas. I'm losing all track of time. I think it must be three years ago. Everything is different now. Even time has changed. It's fractured, like everything else. To think I was even considering moving to France. Where do I get these ideas from? Anyway, I won't knock them as they were good ones. It's just that when one of them takes hold, I find it hard to shake off. Someone who knows something about astrology tells me it's because my moon is in Sagittarius.

Well, look at me now. I've been turned inside out. I'm a different person; more sensitive, more vulnerable, more everything. Life will never be the same again. It would be an affront if it was.

The south of France was a long way for you to travel. You decide to come by train as you'll get to see more of the country and can practise speaking French on the way. I was so looking forward to you coming. Muppet and I were on the platform in good time. You stepped out of the train looking radiant in your jeans, a white shirt and a pale yellow cardigan draped over your shoulders. The bright sunlight and the warmth of the day take you by surprise. You reach in your bag for your sunglasses and a lipstick falls out and begins to roll away. You trap it with your foot then bend down and pick it up. Muppet has spotted you and he strains at the lead, barking. You see him at once and come towards us.

'Hi, Mum. Is everything all right? It doesn't feel like Christmas when it's this warm, does it?' We hug, and you kneel down beside Muppet and pat him.

'Hello, Mupsey. How are you?'

Love,

Mum

20th Jan, 2016, 9.15pm

Jasmine, can you believe it? This morning, I woke up feeling happy and I was full of energy. It's as if I've been zapped with a magic potion that's lasting all day. I take Muppet for a longer walk than usual and find myself smiling at everyone. People smile back. Smiles are infectious. Weather-wise, it's grim out there; however, when you feel like this it doesn't matter a jot.

Carol phones to tell me she is coming to stay. She will want to go out for a bike ride. I'm hoping for another burst of energy like this one as I'd like to join her. I always used to, yet I'm different now. I have far less energy and my body is still full of grief, so everything is hard work and tiring. I won't go to bed just yet as I want this feeling to last as long as possible. I feel at peace with myself. Yes, that's it. I actually feel peaceful. This is very encouraging.

Night night, treasure.

Love,

Mum

8th Feb, 2016, midday

Dear Jasmine,

I'm still in pyjamas and dressing gown and it was like this yesterday. It's okay though, it's just how it is. Tomorrow will be different again. I've been reading about the different stages of grief, however I'm not sure any of it applies. Each day is different and the grief needs tending, so I feel a bit like a shepherd watching over her sheep.

The emotions still course through my body in huge waves, though fortunately they don't last long. They are a bit of a mystery as I have no idea what triggers them. Grief itself is a bit of a mystery. It needs a body to move through for it to gradually dissolve, so when a wave comes I breathe through it, sometimes talking myself through it. You should hear me, Jasmine. Yesterday, I was sitting in the car, breathing and talking to myself. Shoppers were milling around getting on with their own business. Nobody noticed me.

There is a bit more space between the waves these days so it's definitely getting easier. I'm glad because I don't want to carry this grief around for the rest of my life. In fact, I couldn't bear it. I'd rather not exist in survival mode. Even though it's a way off at the moment, I want eventually to feel I am thriving. It's early days, so let's see how this all plays out. If only there were more conversations about grief, there would be much less fear around it. Grief is love that has nowhere to go and it hurts like crazy.

Only three days ago, I met a bereaved mother who

confided that she is nervous about feeling better, because this might be a betrayal of her son who died. I sense her son would be delighted if his mother found a sense of peace and enjoyed some happy times.

Goodness knows how people manage a bereavement when they have to go back to work. The official time off for grief is three days. What nonsense is that!

And how does a couple manage when both parties are grieving, usually quite differently. I guess we have to keep communicating, yet this is hard when you sometimes can't make any sense of what's going on in the turmoil. Goodness, we need support to cope with the craziness and unpredictability of deep grief.

This is just a short note as I know I will feel better for writing. I'll get dressed now as Muppet needs a walk. I'm going to make a big pot of soup later that will last three days. Soup is very comforting.

Love,

Mum

Jasmine,

Today, I'm in a bit of a void and nothing can fill it. I'm in another world to most people and that makes me feel lonely. Loneliness has to be one of the worst feelings of all. Few people mention or talk about you. Yesterday, I met a man at the bus stop who started telling me about his wife who died fifteen months ago. That's similar timing to you. He is still very sad of course. Nobody mentions her name anymore. I tell him all about you and we both feel better for sharing. His bus arrives before mine and he waves from the window. These conversations are precious.

Love,

Mum

Sweetheart,

I'm still feeling lonely, sort of between worlds, yet I sense I am being drawn back into this world a little more. Yoga is freeing my body up. I can't expect someone who hasn't experienced profound grief to understand how it feels. I'm aware that I need friendship and the kindness of others. Please don't turn away or ignore me.

Your visit this morning was very timely. I felt tingling around the left side of my head and down my shoulders. What a joy. Your visit reminds me that even though I can't see you, you are nonetheless close by. You are excited today and suggest I write a book about what I am experiencing.

'It will help a number of people, Mum. I will help you.' I am delighted by your proposal. Yes, we will do this together. What a lovely idea. What with you suggesting I write and my father giving me a golden pen, I think I shall be in good hands.

Muppet is getting very wobbly on his legs, though as you know, he is very determined to keep going. He still manages to go up and down the stairs, even so I sense he hasn't long to live. I can't bear to think of him going. I imagine you will be there to meet him on the other side, and my father may want to be there too.

Love,

Mum

Treasure,

I can hardly believe that Josh has turned eighteen. Where has the time gone? Emma and Charlie arranged a wonderful party for him in the village hall. Everyone turned up of course. They are so good at organising and have clearly put a lot of thought into it. Josh loved every minute and had a speech all prepared. Afterwards, we gave him a huge round of applause and then began playing all kinds of games. The food was great and we all brought our own drinks along. Nobody mentioned you, not even in the speeches, yet I'm sure you will have been there with us.

Emma says you came to visit her a few days ago. She was half awake and half asleep and you lay beside her on the bed. Unable to believe it was you, she asked you to prove it. So you sent her the scent of your jasmine fragrance and because it was so strong there was no mistaking it. Emma wanted more and asked you to do it again. I would be the same. And so you sent her your fragrance again. I'm so glad for Emma that you are clearly wanting to connect with her. You love your sister very much just as she loves you too.

Love,

Mum

Sweetheart,

The days are getting longer, and unlike the first spring after you died, this one is a tad easier. The pains in my ribs are easing. I think massage helps. My ankles, however, are still rather swollen. I know I could do with taking more exercise; however, I lack incentive. Instead of a dog walker, I need a person walker! Maybe when the weather warms up it will get easier. Muppet doesn't need much of a walk though I still take him out. I tend to be up before him these days. Poor old boy, I can't imagine what it'll be like without him, so mostly I don't.

I was overjoyed to feel your presence this morning. You spoke about Muppet and tell me he will remain with me for another six months. Oh, thank goodness I have another six months with him. Dear Muppet. What a chequered past he has had. I am his third owner. When he was two years old, he was found wandering the streets of Gloucester. Some kind person brought him into the animal rescue centre. It's hard to imagine why anyone would abandon such a friendly Shih Tzu. It just so happens that it was day three of my father's search for a rescue dog. When he sees Muppet huddled in his cage, bedraggled and shivering, he knows without any doubt that he is the one.

Muppet settles in well with my parents. My father walks him in the local field and he soon becomes a firm favourite with everybody. Muppet is especially friendly with the dog owners who have treats in their pockets! About three years later, my father has a tumble in the hedgerows surrounding the field. Muppet bounds back to his side, barking frantically to alert the others. Someone hurries over and helps my father to his feet.

About a year later, my father falls over again and this time he is admitted to hospital. The news is grave. He has an aneurysm and even though he is eighty-five, surgery is recommended. I was in Spain at the time, though I managed to get a flight back the following day. We are all there, my mother, my two brothers and I, yet there is one other person missing. It wouldn't be right without Aunt Sarah with us. My father and his sister-in-law get on famously, and after the death of his brother, Sarah and my father kept in close touch. We phone Sarah and she says she will get a taxi at once and be with us in three hours, four at the most. Five hours pass and still there is no sign of her. I go back to the house to find a phone message from the taxi driver. Sarah has obviously given him the wrong address, and although the town sounded similar, it is in fact in the opposite direction to where she needs to be! The taxi driver tells me it will be another two hours before Sarah is with us.

Meanwhile, my father is beginning to lose consciousness as the operation has not been successful. I pat his hands and then his face. 'Wake up, Dad. Sarah will be with us any time now.' He stirs and then closes his eyes again. *Come on, Aunt Sarah!*

At long last, Sarah arrives. When she sees my father, she flings her walking sticks to one side, and as much as she is able, hurries over to his side, calling out to him. My father stirs and smiles faintly and she smiles tenderly at him. They don't need words. It is very moving to witness. Sarah tells my father that she loves him and they say goodbye to each other. My father, who had been waiting for her, then lost consciousness.

I still think about that, Jasmine, and wish we had had the opportunity to say goodbye. We didn't talk about dying and maybe you have to do that for there to be a meaningful goodbye. Although I have struggled with this, I am more accepting of it now.

After the death of my father, the other dog walkers very kindly stepped in to organise a rota to take Muppet out, as my mother was unable to walk any distance. All went well for another two years or so until my mother had a bad fall. She was unable to get herself back to bed, so Muppet curled into the small of her back in a bid to keep her warm. Whether my mother would have survived the night without the warmth of Muppet we will never know.

My mother had been insistent that she wanted to carry on in the house, though after her fall she at long last acquiesced and agreed it was time for her to go into residential care. I'm glad she reached that decision herself.

What on earth shall we do with Muppet? I can't have him as I am off to France soon. I've never had a dog before, cats yes, but a dog would be such a responsibility. In the meantime, we put him into local kennels. Muppet became increasingly miserable. Unable to bear seeing him like this, I sign three forms and then take him home with me. My mother is very pleased with the news and says I may want to keep him. 'Not a chance, Mum,' I tell her.

I have to make a decision about Muppet. It's not an easy one, however, as my heart is set on the trip to France, and I don't feel I can manage it with a dog.

Within ten days of taking Muppet home I decide to advertise him in the local post office: *A loving, well-behaved seven-year-old terrier in need of a good owner.* I barely reach home when the phone begins to ring. A man called Gary wants to meet Muppet so we arrange for him and his wife to come round that afternoon. It is love at first sight for Gary; however, this is all going much too fast for me.

'No, I'm sorry. I can't let you take him home now as I need time to organise his things. Tomorrow will suit better.' I then sit down with Muppet to explain what is happening.

'Muppet, look, I'm going to France soon, and it's not just for a week or two. It will be a longer trip. I've never had a dog before and I really can't take you with me. I'm sorry. I'm sure Gary and his wife will take very good care of you.'

Responding more to the tone of my voice than the actual words, Muppet cocks his head to one side and then the other.

The following day, we are ready to go. Muppet loves the car so he jumps happily into the front seat, his toys, food and bowls, paperwork and the crocheted blanket my mother made him in the back.

For a reason I cannot fathom I begin to cry, and the nearer we get to Gary's house the louder this becomes. I stop the car and then realise… of course, Muppet is a link to my parents and here I am giving him away. You might, Jasmine, think this the perfect moment to change my mind, but I don't. How would I possibly manage a trip to France with a dog, even if that dog is Muppet?

I toss and turn all night long. I know it is too late for regrets; however, the voices clamour on and on in my head. 'What have you done? You've given him away. Your parents' dog...' I am relieved to see the first light of day. The phone rings early. It's Gary.

'Muppet is a lovely dog,' he begins, 'yet our son has developed an allergy to him. I'm so sorry, but I shall have to bring him back.'

Yes, oh yes! Bring Muppet back. He is obviously meant to be with me. Gary brings him over. It's a hot day, and Muppet seems cross and walks straight past me looking for his bowl of water. When Gary leaves, I sit down and apologise to Muppet for giving him away like that. I also promise him it will never happen again. Muppet barks and wags his tail and then goes to the front door. It is time for a walk. And of course Muppet came to France with me.

Love,

Mum

My love,

The weather is weird. It's suddenly turned a bit cold. Lucia reminds me to keep warm and take care of my lungs by drinking hot water with fresh ginger and cinnamon. In spite of gentle stretching and massage, the pains around my ribs and heart are still present. Although I'm used to them, every now and then I get a bit concerned. I reckon I need to sort this, so I've made an appointment with my GP and will ask her to refer me for a chest X-ray. I wonder how you are. You don't have to worry about the cold weather. That must be nice.

Love,

Mum

Darling,

I was nervous I can tell you. In some ways, I didn't want to have a chest X-ray as it would mean having to face up to the results. Do I really want to know whether I'm going to pop my clogs?

After the X-ray, I am shown into the same little room that you and I sat in when we were given the results of your chest X-ray. I can't think about that. I'm so glad it isn't the same doctor though. This man has reddish hair and he speaks with a Scottish accent that is very pleasing to the ear. I could listen to it all day. I ask him how long he's been in the area, and then realise I am trying to prolong the delay before he tells me that he is very sorry but the fact is that I am dying. He picks up the X-ray and holds it up to the light. My heart is going mad in my chest. I wish he would just hurry up and give me the dire news. I also wish there was someone with me as I'll need a shoulder to cry on.

He swivels his chair round and then tells me that my lungs are as clear as the blue skies we enjoyed earlier in the week. He laughs because my mouth is literally gaping open.

'Were you expecting bad news?' he asks.

'Well, yes, I suppose I was.'

Jasmine, I can't believe how HUGE my sense of relief is. I'm so surprised I'm RELIEVED I'M NOT DYING. I'm overwhelmed at how precious my life is feeling. PRECIOUS. Like a gemstone. Does it take a clear chest X-ray when you think you are dying to bring you back to life? Apparently it does. If anyone had dared to tell me after you died that my life would at some point feel precious, I would have told them they were mad. My life has been handed back to me and I'm being asked whether I really want it. I can't remember when I last felt so alive. I've never considered before whether my life has value or not. I think I've taken it all for granted.

The doctor clearly thinks I will be there forever, so he gets up and opens the door for me! I smile and thank him. The corridor no longer seems long and I walk a little faster than usual.

I drive up the hill and stop to let a car pull out. The driver thanks me and I wave at him. Clouds part and little shafts of sunlight break through, streaming over the surrounding fields. I turn into my road.

Love,

Mum

Treasure,

Grief is moving along nicely. There was a lifetime of untapped grief in my body. Repressing my feelings began in childhood. As a child, you don't know what to do with the painful ones, so I got good at numbing them. And in the process, I learned how to act as though I was feeling cheerful.

'Me, down? No way. I'm FINE.'

Numbing the difficult feelings also numbs the lovely ones, such as happiness and appreciation. I didn't know that. So it's more like being half alive, neither really down, nor happy. And what's all this stoic stiff upper lip about? Princess Diana's death blew our stoicism out of the window, so much so that the whole world was wracked with grief. It takes something big for that to happen. Your death is my something big.

I'm feeling more peaceful about what happened between us. The stories of inadequacy I have been telling myself are dropping away as they are irrelevant now. It's the stories that stop the love getting through. My love for you is bigger without them, it's unconditional.

I love you. I wonder if I told you that often enough.

I'm enjoying the yoga classes. The breathing is freeing my lungs as much as the stretching.

Love,

Mum

Dearest Jasmine,

I'm still buzzing after the conference yesterday in Birmingham. I think you would have been proud of me. It was all about how to promote our ideas, so I thought it might be helpful for the book we are going to write. You see I am taking it seriously. I hope you are too!

Being in a racially mixed city was a welcome contrast to the white, middle-class town where I live. And the conference itself was interesting. I had some good conversations which is always stimulating. One of them was with a Jamaican man called James. His kind eyes find me telling him that you died nearly two years ago. I'm doing this a bit more with people, though only when it feels right. James commiserates and then tells me his best friend died recently, and that he has just arrived back from his funeral in Jamaica.

'We believe that it takes nine nights for the spirit of the deceased person to rest and find peace. After that time the burial can take place,' James explains.

'Nine days seems a long time.'

'Yes, though that time is needed. There is always plenty of crying, as well as laughter, music and dancing, and everyone brings food and drink. There were so many people in the house that the road had to be closed as other cars weren't able to get through.' James grins, though he has tears in his eyes.

'That's much longer than a wake in Ireland, which lasts up to three days.'

He nods. 'Here in England there's too much silence around death.'

Even though my mother was Irish, she would never discuss her funeral arrangements, never mind whether to have a wake or not. I rather think that she left some of her Irish ways behind when at the age of twenty-four she married my father. My father, who was an officer in the British army, had just accepted a posting to Egypt, so my mother left Ireland to go with him.

Fortunately, she went back to Dublin as often as she could. I say fortunately because I always loved going there. It was during one of those visits that my mother took me to my first Irish wake. I was about nine or ten. The wake was for a distant cousin who died when he was not much older than you were, Jasmine. The front door was ajar so we let ourselves in. I didn't know what to expect.

The main room is softly lit with two lamps and the coffin is open and on the table. Three women dressed in black are sitting around it. They are the professional mourners whose job is to get the grief moving. They begin moaning and rocking back and forth on their chairs. I'd never seen anything like it before. In fact, I'd never seen a dead body before so I couldn't help staring at this distant cousin who I had never met until now.

In the other room, there's a long table covered with a starched white linen cloth, set with platters of white bread and butter, knobs of jam, homemade cakes and biscuits, and tea served in the best teacups and saucers. It is a veritable feast. Even though people are speaking in hushed tones, it's a bit more cheerful there. One of the men begins to laugh, at which point the whole atmosphere changes. He then removes his hat and starts telling us a story. It's quite an amusing tale. Someone else picks up a fiddle and begins accompanying him with slow, heart-rending music which at times has a little jig mixed in. I came away feeling both captivated and stunned in equal measures.

Jasmine, I'm so glad that after you died, we set aside those few hours to be with you. I would have been left in total shock without them. Why, I wonder, are we in such a hurry to give away the body?

Love,

Mum

My dear Jasmine,

It was lovely having Carol to stay. I was ready for some company. I don't think it's healthy spending too much time alone when you are grieving. You and Carol used to get on well together, and the fact that she knew you makes all the difference to me.

As an ex-professional cyclist, her competitive streak is still alive in her. Usually, she goes out on her own and zooms around the hills first thing in the morning. It is fun to see her reaction when I ask to accompany her on a bike ride, though I have to remind her that I have less energy than she does.

'Shall we go along the canal towpath?' I suggest and she is quite happy with that.

Carol oils the bike chains, checks the tyre pressures and I bring some biscuits and prepare a flask of tea. We are ready to load the car. I like flat areas because it leaves much more space for the sky. We park just around the corner from the canal, then cross over the bridge and decide to turn right towards Gloucester. I am a little nervous as to whether my legs will support my new-found enthusiasm. Oh, what a joy… my legs are moving, the gears are shifting nicely and the bike is responding. What a great feeling! We speed along the towpath, shadows, bulrushes and scudding clouds. I feel like a child, whizzing, then slowing, chilly and then warm, feeling free. We stop for tea and biscuits and a lone swan swims close by. *Are you lonely without your mate?* I want to ask him, or her. I am lonely without you in my life, Jasmine.

The dockland warehouses appear and minutes later the spire of the cathedral, as if beckoning us on. This is proper history, not like the battle dates we had to learn by rote at school. This is alive, old, crumbling, restored and beautiful. We are getting quite carried away with it all. We reach a signpost. It says ten miles and points back to where we started. Impressed with ourselves, we then head back. The wind picks up slightly which makes it harder. Carol speeds on.

'That's fine,' I tell her, encouraging her to go ahead. A few boats are moored, though there aren't many people about. What a great day! Never did I dream we would cycle twenty miles, Jasmine, and even though I may slump tomorrow, that's okay. The up and down of all this doesn't scare me like it used to. Grief is working its way through my body, which means it's on the move and not stuck, and even though I still have some aches, they are manageable. I sense there will be light at the end of this tunnel.

A hot bath with some Epsom salts is the answer now – and then a glass of wine.

Thinking of you, my love.

Love,

Mum

7th Aug, 2016, 11am

Darling,

I knew something was up as my body has been going berserk. It's the lead-up to my birthday and I don't know what to do this year. Talk about psychic connections because then the phone rings. It's Hilary, suggesting that we go away for my birthday, maybe somewhere not too far away. What about Hay-on-Wye, she suggests, as we both enjoy being near water? She's brilliant at finding places on the internet and says she'll get back to me. My spirits lift. I don't know where I'd be without my dear friends.

Love,

Mum

Jasmine,

What the heck's going on? I haven't felt you around for ages. I don't like this one little bit. Okay, so I've become dependent on your signs. So what? WHERE ARE YOU? You haven't made the lamp flicker for ages and I am not feeling you around me like I used to. This is cold turkey and it's too much too soon. The finality of your absence hits me like a punch in the stomach. It's another loss on top of the biggest one ever when you died. I feel so alone. Is this how it's going to be from now on?

I'll go mad sitting around the house so I'm going out for a walk. I decide to walk the four miles into town. I can get the bus back. It's a very pretty walk and the exercise will do me good. Grief has even found its way into my metabolism, so it's up the creek and I've been gaining weight. I only need a light raincoat as the weather is fine. However, halfway there, the heavens open and in no time at all I am drenched through. Fortunately, there isn't long to wait for a bus. Everyone on it is moaning about the weather, yet the weather is nothing compared to how I feel not hearing from you. I trudge upstairs and sit at the back; wet, cold and miserable. The bus rumbles along interminably, stopping at each stop. Passengers get on and others get off. It's so frustratingly slow. I want to scream. And then out of nowhere, I breathe in the distinct and unmistakeable fragrance of jasmine. I wonder if anyone else can smell it. They all seem impervious to it, nearly all of them busy on their phones. I want to shout at the top of my voice, *Can you smell the jasmine?* I don't, of course. Moments later, the fragrance is gone. Did it really happen?

'Just one more time, Jasmine. Please, just once more.'

Ah, there it is again. Thank you. I breathe the heady fragrance deep into my being so I won't ever forget this. Is this it now? Is this the grand finale?

I think you are trying to show me that even when I don't feel you around, it doesn't mean you've gone away. Are you trying to tell me that I don't need any more pictures to fall off the wall, or the lamp to flicker when I'm sad? The fact is that you haven't gone anywhere. We are together and not separate. I put my hand over my heart and gently rub the area. This is where you are now, in my heart. We are one. Then I weep with both the beauty of this and the echo of my loss.

Love,

Mum

My love,

I'm downstairs writing at Mum's desk. I'm so pleased to have it as she used to write letters sitting at it. I miss her greatly.

'This is my red letter day,' she would say whenever I visited, invariably rubbing her hands with glee. I've not heard anyone use that expression since she died. After her death it felt important that a part of her was returned to her homeland, so I took the ferry to Ireland with some of her ashes in a red, plastic urn poised on the passenger seat. Customs waved me through without a second glance. I suppose they are quite used to deceased family members being brought back to Ireland in urns, and even coffins. On the last day, I scattered my mother's ashes in a river beside a well, at the sacred site of Glendalough, where St Kevin, the first Irish saint, founded a monastery.

During those five days, you look after Muppet, and when I get home I find two hearts in the garden made from intertwined willow reeds. Your gift meant more to me than any words. I still have the willow hearts as well as the willow frame you made for the vegetables to clamber up.

The grass needs cutting. I may do it tomorrow. I've opened the back door leading into the garden. The birds are noisy. I love that. Sarah, a dear friend from Canada has been to stay and has given me a present of a large bird feeder. The sparrows have found their way there and they are eating huge amounts. I will have to buy larger bags. Sarah and I go back a long way and there's something very special about that. I love the fact that she comes over regularly, though she tells me that it's time for me to get myself over to Canada.

'Yes, it must be ten years since I was last over.' She shakes her head and asks me to double this number. So you see, I'm not very good at remembering numbers, years and the like, though I know exactly how long it is since you died... it is just over twenty-one months.

The garden is looking wonderful. The jasmine is in full flower and the wisteria has been splendid. I'm sorry to say that the wasteland where you spent so much time preparing a vegetable patch has grown over. I let that go. The wasteland would make a lovely garden. Neighbours and I could share it. We could have flowers, vegetables, a pond... Perhaps more dragonflies would come by.

CAN YOU BELIEVE IT! A golden dragonfly has just flown into the room where I am sitting writing to you. Enthralled, I watch it circle around, then moments later it flies out again. Elated, I follow it outside and watch it hovering around the pond. Then it flies away. You always said that you hoped a pond in the garden would attract dragonflies. This is the first one I've seen, and it couldn't have come at a better time. I can hardly believe it. In a book I have, the dragonfly symbolises *Transformation, magic, and a time of happiness after hardship.*

I smile to myself. The dragonfly is like a messenger from the other side. Thank you! By the way, I'm creating a lovely spot for you in the corner of the garden. I've arranged some pots on your bench. The dolphin stone looks great there and I have hung your sundial on the fence. I hope you like it. I so enjoy sitting by the pond as I can picture you there.

'Come on, Mum. It's time for a cold beer.' I smile and go inside. Yes, you are right. It's time for a beer.

Love,

Mum

Jasmine, love,

I've just returned from a fabulous weekend by the sea with two girlfriends. Oh, I was longing to be by the sea. I realise I need a good dose of sea air every year; otherwise, I don't feel right. The weather was unusually warm; in fact, everything was perfect. Our bed and breakfast is a huge, old house set in large gardens with a pond and a fountain. Their pond is a bit posher than ours!

Our host is an American and he serves us all breakfast outside on the terrace. He loves chatting to everyone. I guess there were about ten of us staying. The combination of smoked salmon, eggs and mushrooms with plenty of tea or coffee is heavenly. You would have loved it.

Since we are in no hurry to leave the garden, our host comes over to join us. However, for some unknown reason, I have dropped into a trough of sadness. I'm on the brink of tears and am thinking of retiring to my room, when one of my friends tells our host that you died just over twenty months ago. He looks terribly crestfallen and then reaches over and touches my hand.

'I'm so sorry,' he says. The genuineness of his sentiments opens me up to crying freely. What a relief, and when I look up, his eyes are also full of tears. I so appreciate his understanding as it means I have no need to hold back the tears. I feel great afterwards.

He then invites us to have another pot of tea and begins

telling us how the garden looked when they first moved in. It has clearly been a labour of love. Their three lively dogs are an intrinsic part of the establishment, and one of them bounds over to sit beside me. I pat him and thank him. He is keeping an eye on me, just like Muppet used to for you.

On Sunday afternoon, we take our leave and thank our hosts for such a wonderful stay. Before I go, his wife tells me that they are in the process of selling up as their business in the United States has gone bankrupt. No wonder he could relate to my loss. You never know what people are holding in their hearts. This will be a terrible wrench for them. You were very much with us all weekend.

Love,

Mum

Oh, this is terrible, Jasmine. Not only is your birthday approaching, but Muppet is worsening. It is nearly six months since your prediction that I would only have him for another six months. I can just about focus on one thing and it has to be Muppet. Emma phones to say that she is putting flowers on your grave for your birthday. Next time I go over, I will clean your gravestone.

I remember the other stones in the cemetery were mostly black, shiny marble with gold lettering. I wanted something more subtle, more discreet, so decided on grey granite with white lettering. We chose the words together. Josh wantedthe word *Beautiful*. Penny asked for *Much Loved* and either Emma or I suggested *Greatly Missed*. So it was *Beautiful, Much Loved, Greatly Missed*.

I don't want Muppet to die on your birthday. I think he is listening to me, because he is rallying a little. I've asked Lucia to give him a treatment. I've never seen her working with a dog before. Muppet responds a bit like I do after a session and is quite playful afterwards. I haven't seen him like this for ages. Lucia and I have a giggle and I make supper for us. It seems that Muppet will not be joining you just yet.

Love,

Mum

25th Oct, 2016, 8pm

Oh, Jasmine,

When Muppet stops eating I know the end is near. I am giving him a little milk and honey – he doesn't want anything else. Even though I know the end is coming, it is still a shock. Yesterday evening, he looked up at me from his basket.

'It's all right, Muppet. You won't have to struggle much longer. Thank you for watching over me for so long. You are a very special dog.'

Muppet is much loved by several children and I'm sure they will want to know what is happening. They all tell me they want to come over and say goodbye to him. They are very brave. The little girl next door is nervous, so she calls in just briefly and leaves crying. A ten-year-old who loves taking Muppet for short walks comes over with her mother and covers him with a blanket. A brother and sister, who together with their parents have looked after Muppet on occasional weekends, make a pilgrimage to the door, each of them wanting a last cuddle with him. They too leave in tears, though they seem to accept that it is his time to go. Saying goodbye has been important for us all.

It's one of the hardest things I've ever had to do. When do I take the decision on behalf of Muppet that enough is enough?

'You will just know,' says someone who knows a lot about dogs. I hope I got it right. I never want to have to go through that again.

Burying Muppet in the garden doesn't feel right. I don't know why. It needs to be somewhere bigger. My brother and sister-in-law agree for Muppet to be buried beneath their enormous cedar tree where he will be joined by a number of other pets – three goldfish, two pet rats, three dogs and four cats, as well as the unfortunate guinea pig who Muppet chased on Christmas Eve. The guinea pig died of shock so my sister-in-law hurried out to the pet shop to buy a replacement. The subterfuge didn't work as you can't fool children that easily!

My brother, sister-in-law and I dig a hole and lay Muppet to rest there. We have a little ceremony and I tell him again how much he means, not just to me, but also to my father and mother.

I drive home on my own. When I get back, next door's bulldog happens to be in the front. Ruby always used to chase Muppet, because as far as she is concerned, she was here first, so this was her territory. Normally, Ruby pays me little attention; however, on this occasion she comes and brushes against my legs, rolls onto her back and then lies across my feet. She is comforting me in her own way, as she instinctively knows what has happened and how I am feeling. Jasmine, our animals never cease to amaze me.

I can't face going inside so I sit in the car for ages. Muppet will not be there to greet me at the top of the stairs, barking his head off. I do hope Muppet arrives safely. He will be very happy to be met by you, and maybe my parents.

Love,

Mum

Jasmine!

It seems I have another visitor! Now that the garden no longer has the scent of Muppet's urine, the coast is clear for any badger seeking a home for the winter. This badger is brazen! He knows the coast is clear and is burrowing a tunnel under the fence. Much worse is the fact that he is digging an even bigger hole under the shed. Considering how much earth he digs out, it's a miracle the shed doesn't collapse. What with the gusty winds we are having and the weakness under the fence, the whole lot blows down. And then the garden gate comes off its hinges and collapses. I stand by helplessly as Boris the badger (as I've named him) continues to dig up the garden in his search for food.

I'm learning a lot about badgers. Apparently, they can sense where the worms are beneath the ground, so their clawing and scraping are far from random acts. One night, at about two in the morning, the automatic light goes on in the garden. When I peer out of the window, I find myself staring into the face of an enormous badger with a long white stripe down the front of his face. He looks terribly fierce! I don't know which of us is the more surprised. Startled, Boris turns tail and scurries back under the shed. He reappears every night in his quest for food, and in the process he tramples on plants and leaves large amounts of slimy faeces in his wake. Little by little, the garden you and I created is being destroyed. Jasmine, I am in despair.

I speak to all kinds of badger-interested people, each of whom tells me the same thing. There is absolutely nothing to be done except ride it out until the spring, when at some point Boris will make his way back to the woods.

Yet despite the havoc in the garden, there is something about the badger's single-mindedness and determination that I can't help but admire, and in some strange, unfathomable way, Boris keeps me going through that first winter without Muppet and the second winter without you. Boris stayed all through the spring.

By early May, the grass resembles a wild meadow. One morning, I look out and a silky brown rabbit is cleaning herself on the grass. So now I appear to have a wild rabbit living in the garden as well as a badger under the shed! When the rabbit hears me, he turns tail and runs down the badgers' hole. When I relay the story to my neighbour, he laughs and says that a badger and a rabbit would never share a home together. Boris must have gone back to the woods.

I tell you, it takes a few weeks to restore the garden and clear away the excrement. I am in touch with a wonderful handyman called Roger who repairs the fence and secures the holes where Boris gained entry.

Roger is an interesting character and is great fun to have around. He tells me he suffered a heart attack two years ago and had to spend five weeks in hospital. During that time he became depressed. His wife brought him in motorbike magazines in the hope of rekindling his passion for bikes and a passion for living, both of which had gone missing. In the six months before the heart attack, Roger decided to sell his motorbike as he was in need of the money. Even though he can't bear being cooped up inside, he gave up working in people's gardens in favour of a better-paid job in an office. In no time at all he became miserable. And then his heart protested.

Six months after getting the all-clear from the hospital and after much reflection, Roger bought himself another second-hand motorbike. He put his suit back in the wardrobe, cut his hair and returned to working in people's gardens.

Roger grins. 'I'm not rich, but at least I'm happy. I couldn't bear the thought of looking back over my life and wishing I had done it differently.' And I am very happy to have met Roger.

Boris no longer has a way into the garden so he will have to find himself another home for the winter. My animal language book says the badger counsels us to be courageous, take a firm stand and speak our mind. I wonder what you would have made of it all, sweetheart.

Love,

Mum

Sweetheart,

It was so nice marking with Emma the day on which you died. She tells me she has put flowers on your grave and the next time I'm over I shall plant some more bulbs. Emma gave me a beautiful bunch of pink lilies and today they have opened a little further. You can imagine their fragrance in the house. Roses and lilies were your favourite flowers, weren't they?

It is three years since you died, and I thought this year's anniversary might feel a little easier than the last. It almost did, except that today I've woken up feeling very low. I miss you terribly. My heart aches with the missing. I never understood the term "heartbreak" until you died. If you haven't had your heart broken, then it's impossible to understand the physicality of it. And what I'm sensing is that painful as it is, after the heart breaks, it slowly begins to repair. In that process, we are taken into the soul of life, into the rich feelings of the heart. I'm on my way, though sense I'm not quite there yet.

Love,

Mum

12th Dec, 2016, 6am

Darling,

I shall probably spend Christmas with friends. Mary has her daughter coming and they have invited me. They tell me I shall be most welcome and in fact the more the merrier. I hope I will be good company. I'm a little nervous. I imagine I will feel wistful seeing a mother and daughter spending Christmas together.

Love,
Mum

18th Jan, 2017, 3pm

Happy New Year, Jasmine! Here we are in 2017.

On more than one occasion, you told me I was too passive. I don't know why but I've been thinking about this quite a lot. You were right. I wasn't sure how to handle other people's anger. Yours erupted a few times and I must admit it used to unnerve me, though I'd be well up for it now! I didn't have any training with feelings when I was growing up. Instead, I learned to bury them. I didn't realise that grieving was the way back to life. So it seems that my search for you was also about finding myself, my true self.

The heart is the feeling centre of the body and is 50,000 times more powerful than the brain. I couldn't believe it when I discovered that. And the heart is the first organ to develop in an embryo in the mother's womb. I've learnt to give my heart as much respect as my brain.

From my heart to yours.

Love,
Mum

25th Feb, 2017, 9am

Darling Jasmine,

I no longer sit on the sofa waiting for you to make the lamp flicker. In some ways, that seems old hat as I know you are with me. I don't need proof anymore. So you may be glad to know that there's no pressure on you to reveal yourself, although if you do, I will of course be delighted!

Emma fell down the stairs recently and has been badly shaken by it. She has been very busy. Goodness, what lengths the body goes to, to get us to cease our endless busyness. She needs a rest, though I'm not sure she will heed her body.

They'll be over next month so I'm looking forward to that. Penny is growing up fast and is already talking about going to university when she leaves school. When I was fourteen I hadn't a clue what I wanted to do. It wasn't until I was forty-two that I applied to university to study psychology. That was my response to being in an empty house after you went off to university. My application was successful. Anyone over the age of twenty four was considered a mature student, which meant that I was doubly mature! I loved every minute of it. Studying, writing essays, chatting with other students in coffee breaks (most of whom were around your age), was such fun. If you remember there was one year when you, Emma and I were studying at the same time. You were up north, Emma was down south and I was in the middle.

Psychology excited me and it also marked a turning point in my professional life. Oh, and I also enjoyed a new relationship, which even though it only lasted a couple of years, gave me the confidence to begin again.

A year later I moved down to Dorset and although it meant leaving old friends behind and a familiar town that I had lived in for twenty years, it was another fresh start. Being near the sea all year round and in a beautiful landscape was very nourishing. I also opened my own private practice.

By far the biggest change in my life has been losing you. It's hard to imagine when you are soaked in sorrow, adrift on a boat going nowhere, that the light will come back and that new beginnings are possible.

I continue to be in awe of how closely our worlds are linked, even after something that seems as final as death. However, nothing can replace the physicality of you. I miss your quirky ways, your messiness and sensitivity, your love of young people and those who are less able to fend for themselves. I miss you being in our world and in my life.

Love,

Mum

Jasmine,

What dreams early this morning! Although they are vividly imprinted on my mind, I shall write them down nonetheless. In the first dream, you are coming towards me bearing gifts. Smiling, you give me a pale green sweater together with a pretty lime-green umbrella with unusual scalloped edges. The gifts are so feminine and are clearly those of a daughter.

The second dream is extraordinary and it is so vibrant I still feel I am there with you. You are in the sea, riding on the back of a dolphin, looking radiant and completely at one with this beautiful creature. Although I want to get on and ride with you, I don't like to ask.

'Come on, Mum. Get up beside me.' The dolphin slows down, you hold your hand out and I clamber up behind you. Although I can't see you or touch your body, I sense you close to me.

I wake up feeling wonderful. Whenever I feel low, I shall take myself back to the dream and remember how it felt riding on a dolphin's back with you. Amazing! Thank you.

Love,

Mum

Darling,

I am so looking forward to a camping weekend with Penny. She has spent a weekend with me on her own, though this will be our first time going away together. I love that my fourteen-year-old granddaughter wants to spend time with me. The feeling is entirely mutual. And there is no one better to go camping with than Penny as she is a very capable Girl Guide who will of course know how to put the tent up!

Love,

Mum

Dearest Jasmine,

Looking back, I see how amusing our camping weekend was, though at one point it felt anything but, I can tell you! Charlie brings Penny to the campsite, halfway between us both. The description of it sounded lovely – woods, farmland, a friendly owner and good facilities. What it didn't say was that the trees made it dark and gloomy, and nearby there is a cage full of noisy, gobbling turkeys! And the owner is far from friendly.

However, we decide to make the best of it and begin putting up the tent. After a few minutes, I discover that half of the tent is missing! It must have somehow fallen out in the cupboard. We have no choice now except to go home. By this stage, I am fighting back the tears. My eternally optimistic granddaughter, on the other hand, thinks we will find the rest of the tent at home. Furthermore, she proposes that we put it up in the garden and pretend that we are elsewhere! And then I remember that we have a very good campsite near me. Perhaps it has a spare pitch.

Not only do we find the remaining half of the tent in the cupboard, we arrive at the campsite in time to be given the last pitch. We have our own fire pit, the showers are clean, our neighbours are not on top of us and the lake is not far away. In short, it's gorgeous.

We have the tent up in no time, the mattresses blown up and a fire crackling. I can't help laughing. It's been quite a day. And then we both start giggling and can't stop. Thinking of it now brings a smile to my face. My granddaughter is wonderful company and very resourceful. Wish you had been there too, though I have a feeling you were with us. You wouldn't want to miss our camping trip now, would you?

Love,

Mum

10th Oct, 2017, 2am

Dearest You,

I can't stop thinking about your birthday. It was very special. I can't believe it is nearly four years since you died. You would have been forty-three.

I picked several of your roses and they are in a vase on the table. Their fragrance is just as strong now as it was in their first year. I shall take myself out for lunch and will walk through the woods to town. If you were here, I would propose going to the fish restaurant as I know you would love it. It's rather expensive so I don't go that often, even though it's well worth it. Today, I'll have the spicy crab soup with fresh bread and butter. It won't be warm enough to sit outside under the willow tree; no matter, as it's very pleasant inside. I shall ask the waitress to leave the table set for two.

Happy birthday, Jasmine.

Love,

Mum

12th Nov, 2017, 5pm

Darling,

There are posters all over town advertising an African three-day grief ceremony in town. I walk past them all as I've had enough grief to last several lifetimes. I'm pretty sure I won't be going, though having said that, the ceremony centres around the teachings of the Dagara tribe in West Africa and as you know I am very drawn to anything to do with the indigenous.

Love,

Mum

Dear Jasmine,

I don't remember when I last slept so soundly. The three-day grief ceremony was very powerful. Yes, I know I said I wasn't going; however, there I am standing in front of a poster in town when a little voice inside says, *Go, just go along and see for yourself.* So I ring up this very nice Australian woman who invites me to come as a grandmother. She tells me that the elders are very important as nothing can take place unless they are present. Well, that's a very different story to what happens over here in our culture. I'm already curious.

Jasmine, I am to be one of four grandmothers and there will be forty participants, with an equal balance of men and women. I like the sound of the mix as so often you only find women doing these things.

Our role as grandmothers is to welcome each person when they arrive and give them a warm hug. Clearly they are relieved to see us, and several come over to say how much better they feel having older women in the group. That is so nice to hear.

We divide into groups and receive instructions to begin building three different focal points. One is decorated entirely in black, with cloths, cushions and candles, another in red and the other in yellow. The black area is where we will take our grief. The red is where we go to honour the ancestors; in other words, anyone who is deceased. You are now an ancestor, Jasmine. I haven't thought of you like this before. I bring along a photo of you to place there and the others do something similar. We all have something or someone we are feeling the loss of. The third area, decorated in yellow, is where we can go to ask for forgiveness, either for ourselves or for others, and call in new beginnings.

Shanah begins by teaching us a simple traditional West African song that will invoke grief in the person who sings it. Throughout the weekend we are accompanied by five drummers who tirelessly and magnificently play a simple yet powerful rhythm over and over again. Only occasionally does one of them get tired and take a break. It's almost magical the way we begin coming together. We are like a real village and before long there is a tremendous sense of belonging. I realise I've been longing for this for a long time. The indigenous create this so easily when they come together. Many of us have neve felt this deep sense of belonging. I have a distant memory of it when I was a four-year-old in Ireland surrounded by aunts, uncles, cousins and grandparents. It didn't last long because my father was in the army so we moved away.

Our grief begins working its magic. In the Dagara tradition, men support the men when they grieve and women support the women. When a man feels his grief rising, he raises a hand and goes into the black area. Another man notices and follows behind him. The women do the same for each other. It is very comforting to know there is someone right behind you who will not leave until you are through. This alone teaches me so much about how it feels to have a person beside you who is not afraid of grief, who may not say very much but who stays with you.

It's an extraordinary sight to see men and women grieving

together; some angry, some crying, some even silent. During the course of the weekend, we grieve as often or as little as the need arises. Most of the time I have no idea what or who I'm grieving for. It doesn't matter. Much of it is for you. But there is more besides, quite a lot more.

By early Sunday evening we are cooked. Nearly everyone has had some major clearing. I feel free and happy. We put on some music and dance our bare feet into the ground, moving towards and away from one another in celebration of what we have achieved together. Then we lie down under blankets to rest and enjoy a little quiet time. Someone in the room begins giggling and before long the happiness spreads. We are all laughing. It is joy, pure and simple. Grief and joy are so closely allied. This never ceases to surprise me. None of us are in a hurry to go home.

I have gained a much clearer understanding of how much richer a community becomes when elders are present. Three young women express their longing to have an older person in their families, and two of them break down in tears. If any of them lived closer, I would offer myself as a surrogate elder.

I hope you enjoyed the weekend as much as I did, Jasmine. I wonder what you made of it.

Love,

Mum

12th Jan, 2018, midday

Dearest girl,

Another year and I'm definitely feeling stronger within. However, when a wave of sadness appears it still knocks me sideways, though fortunately, it is nothing like before. I have learned to be patient as I know it will pass. I miss you terribly.

Love,

Mum

Jasmine,

A combination of cough and cold leaves me feeling rather low.

Unlike Edith Piaf who sings about having no regrets, I have quite a few. Here's one of them...

I wish you had died at my home. We could have moved your bed to face the garden that you helped to make. Anyhow, it wasn't meant to be and instead you went to stay with Emma. It was more sociable being with them. I missed out on so much.

MISSING YOU BIG TIME.

I daresay this will lessen.

Do I want it to?

Will I ever want to leave my cocoon? Will I feel you around me if I do?

Meanwhile, I shall light the fire and stay warm thinking of you.

Love,

Mum

Darling Jasmine,

I had an extraordinary dream last night. My throat was covered with layers of stuff that prevented me from speaking out. I began coughing and coughing and could hardly stop. With each cough, some of it dropped away. My family in Spirit, including you, were around me, cheering me on to write. WRITE. WRITE. COME ON, WRITE!

Okay, I am. I will. Yes!

Then I saw in my mind those football rattles that go round and round making celebratory noises, and there are whoops of laughter all around me. You stay behind and gently rest your head on my lap.

SO BEAUTIFUL

SO CONFIRMING

Thank you.

I love you.

Love,

Mum

Darling,

Sleep evades me. How are you?

I enjoy bringing you into conversations, and when it's appropriate, I share with people I don't know that you died. It is more of a gut feeling who I do this with. I know when I see a light in their eyes that they would like to share their story. Loss becomes more bearable when it is shared.

There is a lot going on here, Jasmine. I'm sad that Ruby the bulldog next door had to be put down. She had been going downhill fast. And with all this rain, the far house has some flooding in the kitchen. This neighbour is experiencing loss of safety. I popped over with some soup. Mind you, her cooker wasn't working so we heated it up on my stove.

Something more cheerful… I saw Emma and family last weekend. I also met your friend Neil in town for a coffee. Were your ears burning? He tells me he still misses you and that your car is going well. His son is four years old now. What a pity you never met him. Neil didn't have a father to parent him. He is doing a fine job as a dad.

Can you believe it, Jasmine? Apparently, the sister of your first boyfriend lives just down the road in the same village as Emma. You and Sam met at school. He was nearly sixteen and you were a year older, and both of you were troubled by the recent break-up of your parents. In spite of Sam's wildness, there was something intrinsically likeable about him. You were perfect for each other and went out together for about a year.

Sam is shocked by the news of your death. He is happily married with four daughters. You were his first love, and he says he has never forgotten you. I thought you might like to know that.

Love,

Mum

6th May, 2018, 8pm

Sweetheart,

Light rain is falling. It's not cold, thank goodness. The lamp has flickered. You only do this occasionally now, but it still makes my heart beat faster. I no longer cry when you make contact like this, so that's progress, isn't it? Your timing amazes me as I was just thinking of you. It's as if you are able to read my thoughts.

I met a bereaved mum yesterday whose daughter died two years ago. She tells me she is unable to shift her sense of despair and has been like it for months. Her breathing is very shallow. It is a bit like yours was when you were in a panic, when all those memories were surfacing. I suggested she try and breathe more slowly and deeply and that it might well help to move the despair. It worked for me. She says she will have a go.

Love,
Mum

Dearest Jasmine,

This may come as a surprise to you but I would like to learn to play an instrument and jam with others. I can't think of anything nicer than people coming together and making music. I mean what could be more heavenly than that? So it's going to be the ukulele, because unlike the guitar I'm told it's quite easy to learn. With just five chords there are a host of songs you can play. It makes me happy playing it and so far I know four chords. There's a ukulele group that meets every fortnight and it's not too far from here. I'll let you know how I get on.

Creativity seems to be the name of the game, Jasmine. I know how important it was for you. Wish you were around big time. Wouldn't we have fun with you playing your guitar and me bashing out a few chords on my ukulele?

Love,

Mum

Darling,

There is not a cloud in the sky on your birthday. It was the fifth birthday since you died so you would have been forty-four. We've had an unusually warm summer and it's carried on into October. Buoyed by the warmth of the day and the deepening colours of early autumn, I decide to go to the lake and bring a flask of tea. There's a lovely patch of grass at the other side so I make my way there. Then, spreading my coat out, I lie in the sunshine, thinking of you.

My thoughts are interrupted when something light brushes my hand. I look down and find myself looking directly into the eyes of a blue and green dragonfly. Its colours take my breath away. After a few moments, it flies off to join a number of others who are swooping and darting around the water. Some have settled on the branches of an overhanging tree, while others hover above the water, waiting to pounce on some unsuspecting insect. Surely they have gathered here to celebrate your birthday. There are so many of them! They represent a time of happiness as well as transformation. I am holding fast to that.

The greens and blues of the dragonflies are the colours you chose for your first painting at school. It was only your second day so you were understandably nervous. You hold my hand tightly and I take you to the classroom door and watch you disappear inside, along with a number of other children, all of whom are probably feeling much like you.

Later in the afternoon, I am there at the school gate to collect you. You run towards me, bubbling over with excitement.

'I want to show you something. It's in the classroom,' you tell me, tugging my hand. Miss Gunn, your teacher, is standing in the doorway with folded arms. She shakes her head.

'Perhaps she could just bring her painting outside to show me?' I venture. And with that, Miss Gunn relents. You bring the picture out, gleaming with pride at the different shades of blue and green that you've splashed on the paper. Maybe that was the beginning of your love for colour, creativity and art in all its forms.

I am so grateful to have your paintings on my walls as they are such an intrinsic part of you, full of life, bursting with colour and energy.

Love,

Mum

16th Nov, 2018, 2.30pm

Dear One,

Please give my love to dad. He would have been a hundred years old today. I've lit a candle for him. His mind was very active right up to the end. I hope I shall be like that. He was playing bridge just a couple of days before his fall, and not long before that he had the ladder out as he wanted to paint a windowsill! My mother went outside, imploring him to come down. Does he pay attention? What do you think? I don't think it's stubbornness, though so what if it is? It's more like determination. You had that and I've got it in me too. So has Emma. It's no bad thing.

Love,

Mum

19th Jan, 2019, 4.30pm

Darling,

I remember you telling me that there are a lot of birds in Spirit and that the birdsong is magnificent. That must be glorious. The days are getting lighter, though you would hardly know it yet.

Sarah is suggesting I go and stay with them in the summer. Now that would be quite a trip flying out to Canada. I haven't seen the home that she moved into after marrying Dave. Their garden overlooks Halifax harbour, which must be lovely.

Five years ago, Dave was still married to Ramona and Sarah was friends with them both. Ramona then became terminally ill, and both Dave and Sarah were present at her end. Some months later, Dave approaches Sarah and asks if she might be able to think of him as more than a friend. Sarah is quite taken aback, and Dave has to woo her for nearly two years. They are very well suited, and it is a joy to see Sarah so happy after all the sadness that preceded it.

We never know what's around the corner.

Love,

Mum

18th March, 2018, 3pm

Sweetheart,

Thank goodness for the faint sun today and the lightening of the days. What a long winter we've had.

When I look in the mirror I would hardly know myself. I see little trace of the woman I used to be. I think you would like my hair, Jasmine. I no longer colour it, so it's white, and I've had it cut short. My hairdresser suggests I put colour on my cheeks and wear bright lipstick, so I do both those things.

Although the signs you used to send have virtually stopped, I know you are with me. Often when I am writing, I feel you as a soft presence around me. I would, of course, give anything to have five minutes with you in person as we would have so much to share. That will have to wait until I get to the other side, though until that time comes, I have an awful lot of living to do.

Love,

Mum

12th May, 2019, 8pm

Jasmine,

I sense that I am coming towards the end of writing to you. It saddens me when I think of this, because something that has been so important to me will be drawing to a close.

Writing to you has been cathartic. It has meant I've faced everything over and over again. This in turn has helped to lessen my grief and also keep it moving through me. I didn't want it getting stuck like it has been in the past.

Emma of course knows I've been writing to you, and she's read one or two of the letters. She doesn't say very much. I wonder how she will feel reading about our relationship. Will she feel a bit left out, or somehow less important to me than you? I hope not, as it would be quite unfounded. I will broach the subject when we meet for lunch next week.

Love,
Mum

3rd June, 2019, midnight

Darling,

I'm late to bed tonight. I've booked my ticket to Halifax. Unfortunately, I have to change planes in Canada, which adds on time to the journey. No matter. I'm greatly looking forward to it. Sarah says she is organising all kinds of things for us to do.

Love,
Mum

Jasmine,

I'm full of jet lag. It's a ghastly feeling, sort of like not being in my body. Sarah was thrilled that I made the effort to go and see her. I've had the time of my life; in fact, I cried at the airport when it was time to say goodbye to them! Dave cooked for us every night so I gave up offering, though instead I did quite a bit of washing-up. They have a spare room where they practise yoga, and it was so nice doing it together. Everything is better doing it together.

They made my birthday so special. Dave prepared a breakfast that was out of this world. I have a photo of it… brown toast with a layer of tomatoes, then spinach topped with a poached egg, all covered in a tasty béchamel sauce.

Sarah is like a fish she's so at home in the water. We swam in Chocolate Lake (!), the sea and another lake where we also went canoeing. The water temperatures were perfect. We bicycled to a nearby concert and afterwards met friends for drinks. Having lived there for nearly forty years, they have a great community of friends. They all seem to look after each other. I'm somewhat envious.

I'd heard a lot about their friends Jane and Michael, so I was very pleased to meet Jane, whose husband, Michael, died nearly two years ago. During the last three months of his life, he said goodbye to each of his friends. Friends in the neighbourhood arranged a rota to cook meals for them so the family could spend more time together. Their three children, who live in different parts of the world, came back and stayed. There was much crying. Their grief, including Michael's, began several months before his eventual death. Jane is doing really well.

Love,

Mum

Jasmine, my love,

I feel so proud of you. You always wanted to get to the heart of something – in fact, you were like a dog with a bone in your quest for truth. From your early twenties, you believed that some kind of trauma had taken place in your childhood. It wasn't until your thirties, when the buried childhood memories began to surface, that a bigger story emerged. Although we will never know the truth of what happened to you, both of us were unwilling to brush those memories back under the carpet. I am sad, however, that it left you with a sense of shame that you didn't have the chance to address. Your cancer put a stop to that. The secrecy of shame is sly and toxic in the way it eats away at our self-worth, obscuring the truth of who we really are. We are all beautiful souls carrying an expression of the Divine within.

This has been an extraordinary journey though grief. I had no idea what it would involve. All I knew was I had to follow it through. Love and grief shattered my heart into a million pieces, and in some dark, forgotten places I was broken apart and remade.

It is time now to return to the outer world. When I remember how at one point I did not want to live, I am amazed at how far I have come. Grieving is a fast track back to life. I am changed, transformed and passionate about life in all its forms. Thank you Jasmine for making contact with me when I was desperate, for not giving up on me, for teaching me about the world of Spirit and showing me that life doesn't end after death.

When I was raging against God beside the lake, it was such a surprise to discover that I felt so abandoned. I know now that it was not God, the Creator, who abandoned me. It was me who separated from God, because my sense of shame and guilt had me believing I wasn't worthy of being loved. I didn't think I was good enough, intelligent enough or beautiful enough. On and on. NOT ENOUGH! At times, even receiving something simple like a compliment was hard. It's much easier to give than it is to receive. Dear oh dear. How sad.

On the whole, this is now a thing of the past. Instead of tending to others first, I lean in towards myself. I am kind to my dear self. I no longer feel the need to please others in order for them to like and respect me. Occasionally, when I am tired, the old patterns begin creeping back. There's a bit of a game going on between us, but after a few words they soon scurry away!

For years, my body and my feelings were frozen. No wonder I couldn't make sense of what they were. Your death blew away my defences. My feelings and emotions reared up with such a sense of longing to be heard and felt. I see now how precious they all are. I listen to my feelings and they gradually dissolve.

My search for you began some years before you died and of course it continued after your death. And then you came and found me! And through grieving I found myself.

No one tells us that grief is a call back to our inner world. The indigenous know this, and they honour and respect the person who is feeling their grief for they truly understand the profundity of the grieving process. However, for many of us, our underworld is unknown and therefore scary. We don't know where it will take us, so not surprisingly we do anything to avoid it. The mind is then free to have its way with us, and it will keep us going round and round in circles.

Grief has huge power and potential if we allow ourselves to be supported and swept up in her arms, carried into uncharted territories. There is so much to discover about ourselves. Perhaps we might dare to not push grief away, be it our own or that of others.

Thank you, beloved daughter. Grief has been a gift.

Love,

Mum

Darling,

Another birthday. How time is passing. It is nearly six years since you died. You would have been forty-five.

We have done this together. Thank you for being with me every step of the way. Gratitude to my father also, and to all my ancestors who stand in the wings cheering me on. I love knowing that you are all there. My love to you all.

Our task is complete and the book is written. I'm pleased it will be going out into the world.

I have moments of desolation when I imagine you might disappear, yet I'm sure you won't. My grief is still moving, though now there is deep joy underneath it. The joy of life.

I look forward to new beginnings, for I know they will surely come.

Loving you always. Until we meet again.

Love,

Mum

Sorrow prepares you for joy. It violently sweeps everything out of your house, so that new joy can find space to enter. It shakes the yellow leaves from the bough of your heart, so that fresh, green leaves can grow in their place. It pulls up the rotten roots, so that new roots hidden beneath have room to grow. Whatever sorrow shakes from your heart, far better things will take their place.

Rumi

Acknowledgements

To indigenous cultures everywhere, deep gratitude for the way you uphold your customs and protect your lands. It is because of you that we are reminded what it is to be human.

To the friends along the way who read and encouraged me with their feedback: Chris Haskett, Sophie Bennett, Helena Foss, Christina Pockett, Lucia Victor Jayaseelan, Joan Gill, Alice Campbell, Robin Badham-Thornhill, Sue Edwards, Amanda Relph and Catherine Ross, thank you all so much.

Sarah Wakely coached me on the correct use of tenses and punctuation, and the observational skills of Hamish Ross were invaluable. Thank you, both. To Margaret Koolman, deep gratitude for the final proof read.

Thanks are due to the Marist Sisters in Nympsfield, who in the second year offered me a place to write when I was in need of extra holding.

Enormous thanks to Shanah Rivers, who introduced me to the grief ceremonial work of the Dagara tribe, based on the work of Malidoma Patrice Somé.

Thank you Sheddy, for your photography and generous spirit; Jessy Plant, thank you for your artwork; and to Jessica Pilkington, my thanks for your PR input.

The diligence, invaluable comments and clarity of Ruth Foulkes enabled me to better understand the issues surrounding trauma. Thank you so much.

Christina Pockett and Brian Foulsham redecorated my

office when the book was stuck and got me going again – thank you, both!

To Hilary Franklin, for all you have taught me about ceremony, and for your unbridled constancy, wisdom and love – thank you.

To Marge Moseley, for your constant presence of friendship and deep wisdom when I kept asking you to read more – thank you.

Enormous thanks are due to the editorial work of Tigga Goode and Sue Brayne; and deep gratitude to Angela Clarence, who with humour, patience and a gentle touch, insisted that I not soften the story.

And finally, my thanks to Matador who helped me to let go of the book in order that it may find its way into the world.

ABOUT THE AUTHOR

Born in Dublin, Patsy Freeman initially trained as a state registered nurse. In her early forties she gained a degree in psychology. She holds an advanced certificate in counselling, and has worked with patients in a GP practice in a trial to assess the benefits. She then opened her own private practice. Patsy lives in Gloucestershire and, since the death of her daughter in 2013, gives inspirational talks on the healing powers of grief.

www.patsyfreeman.com

AQA Biology

2nd Edition

A LEVEL
YEAR 1
AND AS

HAMPTON SCHOOL

Name	Form	State	Date	Initials
Robert Morey	L6AHJ	N	6/9/18	RJD/HSM

State   **N** New   **A** Good   **B** Fair   **C** Poor

HAMPTON SCHOOL
BIOLOGY DEPARTMENT

Glenn Toole
Susan Toole

OXFORD

UNIVERSITY PRESS

Great Clarendon Street, Oxford, OX2 6DP, United Kingdom

Oxford University Press is a department of the University of Oxford.
It furthers the University's objective of excellence in research,
scholarship, and education by publishing worldwide. Oxford is a
registered trade mark of Oxford University Press in the UK and in
certain other countries

British Library Cataloguing in Publication Data
Data available

978-0-19-835176 4

10 9 8 7 6 5

Paper used in the production of this book is a natural, recyclable
product made from wood grown in sustainable forests.
The manufacturing process conforms to the environmental regulations
of the country of origin.

Printed in Great Britain by Bell and Bain Ltd, Glasgow

Message from AQA

This textbook has been approved by AQA for use with our qualification. This
means that we have checked that it broadly covers the specification and we
are satisfied with the overall quality. Full details of our approval process can be
found on our website.

We approve textbooks because we know how important it is for teachers and
students to have the right resources to support their teaching and learning.
However, the publisher is ultimately responsible for the editorial control and
quality of this book.

Please note that when teaching the *AQA AS or A-Level Biology* course, you must
refer to AQA's specification as your definitive source of information. While this
book has been written to match the specification, it cannot provide complete
coverage of every aspect of the course.

A wide range of other useful resources can be found on the relevant subject
pages of our website: www.aqa.org.uk.